Praise for

"Chris S. Reynolds understands that happiness must be found in the journey; it is not the prize at the end of the journey. In *The Six Circle Strategy*, he shares years of learning for entrepreneurs starting out or looking for further success. In short, he provides a road map for your own entrepreneurial journey and happiness."
JAMES O'SULLIVAN, president and CEO of IGM Financial

"*The Six Circle Strategy* is filled with real-life examples that are built on timeless principles that will work for you if you put them to work. Anyone interested in bringing the best out of themselves and their enterprise will benefit greatly."
MITCH ANTHONY, author of *The New Retirementality*

"The problem for most aspiring entrepreneurs is not a lack of a desire but the inability to get started. Chris S. Reynolds provides not just the self-awareness needed to act but brilliant, impactful strategies to ensure success becomes sustainable. Highly recommended."
SANDRO FORTE, entrepreneur, global speaker, and author of *Dare to Be Different*

"*The Six Circle Strategy* isn't just another business book. It's a straight-talking, story-rich framework for building a business that doesn't burn you out. If you want wealth, freedom, and fulfillment without losing your soul, read this."
MARCUS SHERIDAN, international keynote speaker and bestselling author of *They Ask, You Answer*

"If you want to build your business, it is simple: put people first. *The Six Circle Strategy* takes you step by step to achieve your dreams and goes full circle."

PATTIE LOVETT-REID, former chief financial commentator for CTVNews and bestselling author of *Live Well, Retire Well*

"*The Six Circle Strategy* amplifies the imperative for entrepreneurs to look inward to explore a deeper understanding of why freedom remains their most intoxicating dream. Beautifully conceived and written. I devoured this classic-in-the-making in one delicious bite."

TOM DEANS, speaker and award-winning author of *Every Family's Business* and *Willing Wisdom*

"Wealth isn't just what you earn—it's how your entire life works together. *The Six Circle Strategy* offers a revolutionary framework for financial advisors and clients alike to build meaningful, sustainable success. The result? Clarity, confidence, and a richer life in every sense."

DR. DANIEL CROSBY, *New York Times*-bestselling author of *The Soul of Wealth*

"Packed with lived wisdom and real-world strategies, *The Six Circle Strategy* is a refreshingly honest guide to building wealth and freedom. Chris S. Reynolds draws on deep experience to deliver actionable steps that apply whether you're in wealth management or any field. In addition to the advice to 'trust what you're paid to do,' this book offers a clear, practical road map to create lasting success."

GREGG BROWN, speaker and *New York Times*-bestselling author of *Spark Action*

"*The Six Circle Strategy* builds on real-world experiences that lead to a set of guiding principles for entrepreneurial success. It's an effortless read with a wonderful mix of personal stories and evidence on what it takes to design and achieve a powerful vision for the future."
JULIE LITTLECHILD, founder and CEO of Absolute Engagement

"*The Six Circle Strategy* is a refreshing and inspiring guide for entrepreneurs who want more than just financial success—they want a life filled with purpose, freedom, and fulfillment. It's a must-read for anyone who wants to build not just wealth but a life they truly love."
GEORGE HARTMAN, president and CEO of Market Logics and author of *EXIT Is NOT a Four-Letter Word*

"This is a must-read for any entrepreneur seeking a pathway to success. *The Six Circle Strategy* serves as a foundational blueprint to both professional and personal success by revisiting one's choices, identifying necessary changes, rebuilding skill sets, and adapting to the opportunities ahead."
NICK PSZENICZNY, executive chair of Advice Canada and Financial Horizons

"Accessible, thought-provoking, compelling, and entertaining. Chris Reynolds's journey and insights will help you frame how to realize your own version of success. This is an important read from a leader who achieved ambitious goals through client-centricity, building teams with complementary skills, and not compromising on the things that matter."
LUKE GOULD, president and CEO of Mackenzie Investments

Hey Daniel,
Thanks for all your Support.

THE SIX CIRCLE STRATEGY

Live Your Dream!

Hey Daniel,

Thanks for all your support!

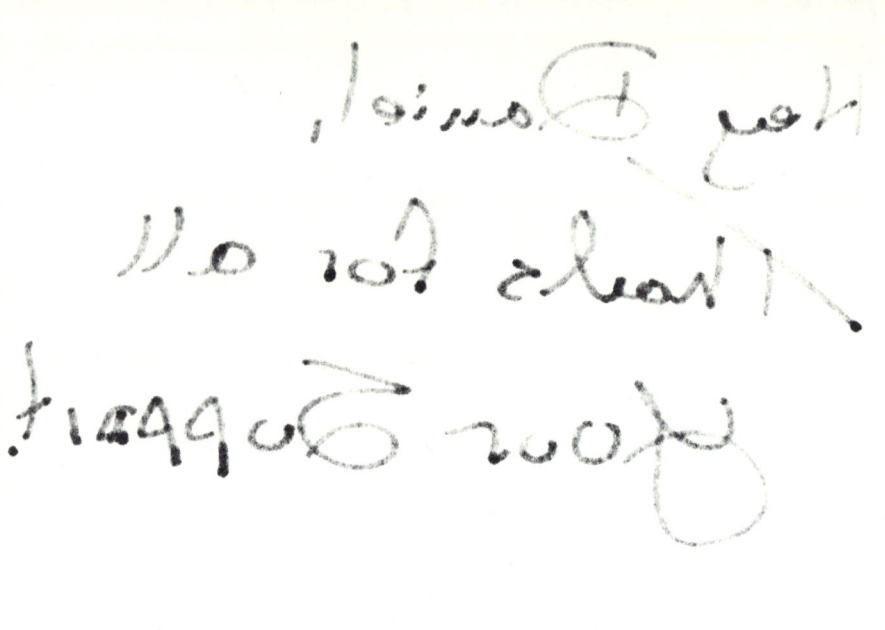

The Entrepreneur's Journey to Wealth and Freedom

Give you bloom!

THE SIX CIRCLE STRATEGY

CHRIS S. REYNOLDS

PAGE TWO

Copyright © 2025 by Chris S. Reynolds

All rights reserved. No part of this book may be reproduced, stored in a retrieval system or transmitted, in any form or by any means, without the prior written consent of the publisher, except in the case of brief quotations, embodied in reviews and articles.

Some names and identifying details have been changed to protect the privacy of individuals.

Cataloguing in publication information is available from Library and Archives Canada.

ISBN 978-1-77458-591-7 (paperback)
ISBN 978-1-77458-592-4 (ebook)

Page Two
pagetwo.com

Page Two™ is a trademark owned by Page Two Strategies Inc., and is used under license by authorized licensees

Cover and interior design by Cameron McKague

chrissreynolds.ca

*I learned this, at least, by my experiment;
that if one advances confidently in the direction
of his dreams, and endeavors to live the
life which he has imagined, he will meet with
a success unexpected in common hours.*

HENRY DAVID THOREAU, WALDEN

Contents

0 Move in the Right Circles *1*

CIRCLE ONE VISION

1 Listen to the Tycoon Cowboy *9*

2 Fall in Love *15*

3 Get on Your Quest *21*

4 Be Like Arnold *29*

CIRCLE TWO TRUST

5 Find Your Plumbers *39*

6 Solve Obvious Problems *45*

7 Decide If You're Pete's Donuts or Tim Hortons *51*

8 Open the Window *59*

CIRCLE THREE FOCUS

9 Don't Mess with Success *69*

10 Outsource Catching Rabbits *75*

11 Read the Book *81*

12 Follow the Road to Japan *89*

CIRCLE FOUR VALUE

13 Map the Little Things *99*

14 Communicate Constantly *105*

15 Provide the Greatest Client Experience *113*

16 Answer Before They Ask *119*

CIRCLE FIVE RELATIONSHIPS

17 Create Deep Relationships *129*

18 Don't Manage People *137*

19 Keep Raving Fans, Drop the Rest *143*

20 Sustain Yourself *149*

CIRCLE SIX FULFILLMENT

21 Put People Before Everything *159*

22 Scale Like Schultz *165*

23 Put Passion Before Work *171*

24 Roll Forward or Roll Back *177*

25 Remember the Circle of Life *183*

Acknowledgments *187*

Notes *189*

0

Move in the Right Circles

WHY IS this chapter 0? Because everything starts with circles, and everything circles back.

When we imagine a journey to entrepreneurial success, we often picture it following a straight line from the outset. That line is marked by a series of steps to get from here to there. We rely on these kinds of lines everywhere in business: profit-margin graphs, business life cycles, and project-schedule charts. We want that line to steadily move upward.

As a successful wealth management entrepreneur, I have learned that the reality of the business world is much less straightforward. After all, entrepreneurship isn't just about starting a business—it's about running one. Everyone who wants to achieve something great in life experiences side journeys, setbacks, and opportunities. We have to be ready for the curves that business throws at us.

We need to recognize that to get to our best, we have to constantly revisit our choices, change and rebuild our initial skill sets, and come back to our clients. It's a process of incremental change, and that means looking both forward and backward simultaneously. Entrepreneurship is a long game, and it requires us to create clear boundaries between what we want and can do and what we should leave to others.

That's why entrepreneurship, if it's done well, is all about circles. A circle is the shape of a lens that helps you focus on what matters. It's also the most efficient, economical shape: the least perimeter for the most area.

And life, as we all learn, also goes in circles. Your family circle, your circle of friends, your business circles—they all exist within the sun's ring of the day, the moon's ring of the month, the Earth's ring of the year. Past, present, and future connect in a circle.

This book connects my past, our collective present, and your future.

When I was young, my knowledge of money was based on how my own family operated. My father ran a thoroughbred horse farm, and my mother came from a long line of academics. Academia is an honorable endeavor, but one focused on the bliss of expanding human knowledge, not building capital. And while there was some money in thoroughbreds, it was a physically and mentally demanding life built on the love of those extraordinary animals more than anything. So I didn't learn much about money, at first. But I learned about circles.

Raising thoroughbreds is an exercise in learning about circles. If you've ever seen a horse race, you know they run in counterclockwise circles. From working with my father, I learned that you have to train horses in circles from the time they're born so that they get used to the pattern. A well-developed horse training program is an exercise in following the art of the circle.

Circles require a horse to be obedient and engaged. They teach a rider to be accurate and precise, subtle in cues, and centered in the saddle. The circle is a pattern that is both easy to trace and difficult to perfect. Learning how to move in circles is a beautiful thing.

From my days at the track onward, my life has been full of circles. The coins in my pocket—which I never had enough of as a kid—were circles. The sun in Florida—where I wanted to live—was a circle. The dial on the phone I used to sell insurance at my first desk job was a circle. The cul-de-sacs and crescents in the suburban neighborhood where I first built up my wealth management business were circular. The clocks that measured the time I was spending (well or, sometimes, badly) in the office were circles. The cappuccino cups I always welcomed my clients to the office with were circles. The wedding ring on my finger is a golden circle. The world I've traveled around for leisure and adventure is a huge, ever-growing circle.

But there are less concrete circles too, and it's those that have kept me on track in my life. This book is about the six interlocking circles that have been my strategy for success over the past thirty years of building, buying, growing, and selling my own businesses as a wealth management entrepreneur.

Circle One: Vision. Building wealth doesn't start with strategy. It starts with connecting the dots between self-awareness and vision.

Circle Two: Trust. If you want to find clients and customers, turn away from the big blue ocean and look for a small blue pond where you can see and know everyone, and they can see and know you.

Circle Three: Focus. Ramping up the complexity of your business dissipates your energy. Focus in on a simple solution.

Circle Four: Value. To create value for your clients and customers, you have to authentically value them, their time, and their experiences.

Circle Five: Relationships. You absolutely must develop deep personal relationships. Your clients, team members, and suppliers need you to be emotionally mature and lead generously.

Circle Six: Fulfillment. Focus on what makes you and your clients feel fulfilled, not just satisfied.

Whether you're in the wealth management business or some other line of work, the same rules apply. Let me tell you my story and the stories of the people who've inspired me the most, and I think you'll come around to seeing what I mean.

CIRCLE ONE

VISION

THE FIRST circle that matters is your eye, because the first thing you need to do is home in on a target. You need a vision. You need to be able to see what it is you want.

What *do* you want most?

Do you, above all, want to work for someone else for a living? Or do you want emotional, creative, and financial independence?

If you're an entrepreneur like me, your vision is set on independence.

When I started my first business, I didn't have a grand vision. I had a few good partners and we all had our own skills, but there wasn't an overarching plan in place. We didn't fail at growing our respective business interests, but we never really became a cohesive team and ended up going our separate ways. That's *too much* independence, because if you're going to think big, you'll need more than one person to actualize your plan.

Entrepreneurs aim to cultivate the means to support themselves and others. Steve Jobs, the founder of Apple, was famous for getting world-class talent to do extraordinary things by sharing his vision for his organization. If you know his story, you've heard countless examples of Jobs getting his team on board to make his vision of what's possible a reality. He wanted to change the world, and change it he did.

Most people will get worn out and stop trying, start making excuses, and let themselves quit while they're behind. But you're allowed to create a vision that inspires *you* on your journey, not just others. Your vision can be an idealized version of how you'd like to imagine your future—not just an action plan. I know from my own experience that if you are truly passionate about your vision, it will see you through to success.

Maximum effectiveness and minimum effort are your goals when perfecting a circle. Riding in a perfect circle, for example, enhances horsemanship because it's the ultimate test of the animal's direction, gait, and speed, and the rider's ability too. The same is true for business. And making a plan that is both effective and effortless starts with your Circle of Vision. To create a vision that works, you have to start by knowing yourself: understanding your interests and goals, as well as your skills. It starts with aligning your self-awareness and vision so that you can map out your quest to success.

It starts with you.

1

Listen to the Tycoon Cowboy

AT WOODBINE, the tycoon cowboy always came in late. He was one of the most successful horse trainers in Canada and the United States, and he followed his own mind and no one else's. I might have arrived at six in the morning, but he was more likely to saunter in at ten. As soon as he hung up his coat, he grabbed himself a cup of coffee and walked around to talk to his staff and look at the horses. A little while later, you could see him lean back at his desk, read the paper, and write in the journal he always kept in his back pocket.

I was still in high school, but I needed the cash—and I loved working with horses. And Woodbine Racetrack was a great place to get high-level experience. Woodbine is a thoroughbred horse racing facility on the outskirts of Toronto. It's the latest iteration of a track that, since 1874, has been a place to find people who move in rich and powerful circles, figuratively speaking—and horses that do the same, literally.

All horses know how to run, of course. But in the wild, they run to get from one place to another. On racetracks, they run on course, in a circle, to get back to where they started. And that's something they need to learn how to do. They need to understand how to channel their energy effectively around that circle for the whole race.

Watching the tycoon cowboy, I knew I wasn't on *any* track yet. I certainly didn't belong on a thoroughbred circle track. A vital part of a horse learning to run is mastering how fast they can get out of a starting gate. They have to learn to exit the stall at a run. As for me, I was still learning about how to step *into* the gate. But I was a curious guy. I started observing what the horse trainer did all day, counting the hours he put in on what he was paid to do, namely training horses (and spending time with horse owners, developing relationships with them). What he did differently from other trainers, strangely enough, was work less.

There was a big gap between the number of hours that the tycoon cowboy put into his job and, say, the number my father spent on the farm. My father was a proud workaholic, and all he seemed to get from this hard work was exhaustion. By contrast, this highly successful trainer hardly did anything.

This confused me. I had to ask him what the deal was. I figured that it couldn't hurt to ask the tycoon cowboy why he was so successful with so little effort.

"Use your head, not your body," he told me. "The simple math is this—from the neck down you might be worth a hundred thousand dollars, but from the neck up you're worth untold millions."

Then he broke it down for me further.

"Too many people think work is about your body, but if you can, you should find a career where you are paid to think.

If you rely on your body and your body wears out, you'll limit the amount of potential that you will ever have. But if you use your head, you can inspire, motivate, and lead other people to help you build your vision. You then can multiply your success, and that success can go on forever."

That idea changed my life. With his advice in mind, I started to create my Circle of Vision—my image of who I wanted to be and how I might get to where I wanted to go in life.

I knew I had a serious dislike of northern winters and wanted to live in Miami. *Miami Vice* made the city look cool—its protagonists had the suits, the cars, the nightlife savvy. To get there—or anywhere, frankly—I figured out pretty quickly that I had to find the time and build the financial acumen to create the life I wanted.

In every way I could imagine, I started to use my head.

I started to read everything I could get my hands on about businesses, successful people, and money. The tycoon cowboy wasn't wrong: Successful people focused on what was possible, then built a team to bring their vision to life. Steve Jobs didn't engineer his own products, but his vision inspired people to change the world. Bill Gates was a gifted programmer, but Microsoft wasn't built by him alone—it was created by bringing together a group of people focused on one mission, creating a new operating system. The same can be said of Oprah Winfrey or Richard Branson or Warren Buffett: They know what they do best, and delegate or share the rest.

Based on what I learned, I decided to create a career as an entrepreneur.

FROM ONE simple, single piece of advice shared with me on a thoroughbred racetrack, I learned that the only real commodity we have is time, and how we use it is crucial to our success.

We can trade time for many different valuable things.

We can trade time for money, as we do when we work for other people. That's the most straightforward path, but it isn't one I'd recommend.

We can trade time for meeting people who may connect us with new ideas and opportunities. I have had the opportunity and privilege to work with and learn from highly talented people. I am a big fan of standing on the shoulders of giants and learning from other people's trials and tribulations. I can think of hundreds of pieces of advice I have received throughout my life. Some of this advice was good, some bad, and some I wish I had listened to more closely.

We can trade time for learning skills through reading, taking courses, and trying out a range of roles. Reading made me change my entire viewpoint on how to create value: by using the skill sets of other people to build a company. But learning horse farming was just as valuable. Every experience you collect is a chance to connect the dots between what you imagine for your future and how you achieve that.

But, most valuable of all, we can trade time for creating new ways to solve problems. That's how any business or personal project succeeds. How do we decide how much time to spend on what we do next? Sure, we all want to spend more of our work time using our minds and less using our bodies, but that can look different for each of us.

Each of us has to start with our own simple time equation. I'm not talking about time management. We have planners and calendars for that. I'm talking about your vision for yourself and the time you have to spend in your lifetime.

We have to have a clear vision of what matters to us from the very beginning of our entrepreneurship journey. If we're not listening to ourselves, then we're following other people. Doing that is a setup for failure as an entrepreneur for the simple reason that when we're following, we're not leading.

So let's start with your vision for your time. Consider these five questions:

How do you spend your time right now? Like the tycoon cowboy, I value independence. I don't like following set rules, but I do have an enormous amount of discipline. That means I'm ready to dive deep when I need to, and I'll follow an idea through to its completion.

What do you want to do all the time? I love people. I love talking, listening, and learning from people. That's what I value the most, so that's what I spend my time doing.

What do you never want to spend time on? I never want to be a workaholic, and I don't want to feel like I can't take a vacation. I value my personal time.

Are you currently getting the results you need from the time you're spending? If I'm not getting the results I want, I go back and think hard about where the gaps might be in my current time equation.

How can you help yourself shift your time equation to a value equation? Is the time you're spending worth the value you're receiving? For me, this is where the rubber meets the road. I look at what I'm craving to spend time on and evaluate what to do next. If I'm doing too much heavy lifting with how I spend my time, I know that something has to give.

You can't afford to waste time on activities that don't ultimately bring you joy. Take some time to reflect on what your time means to you. Your potential for success won't be there forever, so the time to start is now.

2

Fall in Love

If you're not fully in love with what you do for a living, you can't become a successful entrepreneur.

Why? There are a few obvious reasons.

If you're working for someone other than yourself, you're likely working harder and for longer hours than you'd like. If you don't love what you do, those hours probably feel lost forever.

If you're already an entrepreneur, you're likely working harder and for longer hours than you'd like—but without a guaranteed income. If you don't love what you do, you're setting yourself up for eventual failure because your interest and drive will peter out.

If you're already a successful entrepreneur, you're likely working harder and for longer hours than you'd like, but *with* a guaranteed income. But if you're reading this book, you're looking for ways to improve your work life, which means you're not in love with what you do. You're likely going to bail sooner rather than later.

No matter which of these applies to your own situation, the same wisdom applies: Every day is either an investment in yourself and your future, or a waste of your very valuable time.

Here's the problem with all of these career options, however. A lot of people believe they can't fall in love with what they do at all. In fact, researchers have found that adults fear they'll never get passionate about work, and therefore feel they have nothing to lose when they leave a job or give up on their entrepreneurial dream.

But there's a flaw in that logic. A big one.

The same researchers found that it's the belief and not the passion that's at issue. They conducted another study in which 700 adult undergraduate students were given reading and writing activities that helped them think about interests and passions as cultivated, something that could be developed rather than acquired in a burst of inspiration.

All of these students were registered in the Faculty of Arts but were required to take either a math or science course by their university. By the end of the year, the students who took part in the study were more interested in their required math and science courses than those who didn't—and this boost was particularly apparent among students who initially reported that they were not a "math-and-science person." They also earned better grades in those courses in comparison to those in the control group. These students, who might have otherwise ignored the courses altogether, became more skilled in math and science, and according to the research team, they also grew into interdisciplinary scholars.

All it took for this change to happen was for these students to believe they could become passionate about something they had previously hated spending time doing. None of these students ever saw themselves as numbers people; they saw themselves as communicators, artists, psychologists. They only created new values for themselves when they were prompted to consider what math and science could add to their futures.

I DIDN'T love long hours of hard physical work. So I decided to trade that for work using my mind. I started in insurance, but really I was a glorified telemarketer. When I arrived for my first day on the job, my boss gave me a phone book.

"Here's your book of leads," he said. He dropped the heavy brick of paper on my desk, turned around, and headed back to his office.

The company didn't even give me a script. And no one could say the job itself was inspiring; it wasn't. But I refined my pitch, then refined it again, then refined it once more. I sold some insurance and eventually did well, and the reason I did well isn't because I was passionate about insurance itself. It was because my job involved talking to people all day long, and I was passionate about them. I happen to love people, which is why I love every day I spend supporting, educating, and just being with people. I learned about the insurance products so that I could do what I loved, and get better at it.

The company did have really good insurance products, which can be an integral part of a person's portfolio. But I wouldn't have put pressure on myself to learn more, do more, and be more for my clients if I wasn't passionate about their lives and what they needed to make their futures a little safer, a little more secure. I like to see people do better and thought I could help them. Because I was so passionate about my clients, I didn't really think about being rejected as much as I focused on the positive impact of my work. Over time, as my clients became more successful, I saw that I was changing lives.

I fell in love with my customers, and I'm still in love with them. And knowing about insurance was also a gateway to learning about mutual funds and the next stage of my career. I've repeated this same pattern ever since, becoming an expert in something that I know helps other people.

Unlike the subjects of the study on cultivating interests, I didn't go to university. Nor did I follow in my mother's footsteps any more than my father's. But I did follow the approach suggested by that university study. I reflected on the thing I valued in a job that I didn't, at first, fully understand. I built a passion around that part of the business and did what I could to support that passion. Focusing on it was central to my success.

If you can fall in love with your work, that's the first step to feeling good every day for the rest of your life.

Now, you can either build a business that will sustain your lifestyle, or you can wrap your lifestyle around a business and work yourself into the ground. If you're always feeling like your work is drudgery, you're always going to be putting too much of your energy into sustaining your daily grind. In fact, you'll end up feeling exactly the same as you would if you were performing manual labor: Your mind and body will be overloaded with stress, and you'll set yourself up for burnout.

In finding the one key thing that I loved about my work and remaining true to that passion, I started to connect the dots. What my clients wanted and what I wanted for myself were the same thing: a better kind of life, one that didn't feel as difficult, as complicated as life often seems to be. There were a lot of paths available to us, but if I could excel at my job, I knew I could create happiness for all of us.

To build my Circle of Vision, I had to not only believe in myself, build my skills, and earn my clients' trust.

I also had to discover my lifelong path.

3

Get on Your Quest

ONE NETFLIX binge night, I had a revelation.

I was watching an episode of *The Sandman*, the show about the mythical character Morpheus. He's the personification of both dreams and nightmares. Although the show's Morpheus is a new incarnation, he's based on a figure in Greek literary mythology who can tell human beings their future through their dream state.

In *The Sandman*, Morpheus must go on a series of adventures to get back his power. He overcomes all the obstacles set in front of him, but when he has done it, he is sad. He is asked about his sadness and glumly replies that nothing is exciting to him any longer. Morpheus has no reason to get up in the morning.

Suddenly, something clicked for me.

Morpheus was at a loss because without new obstacles, new adventures, new demands to make him feel important, to feel challenged, to feel needed, he felt like his life was pointless.

I thought back to the period in my own life when I didn't feel challenged. This was before I knew what I wanted to do with my time, before I recognized the thrill I could get out of an entrepreneurial life. And without challenge, my interest in my life waned, just like Morpheus.

What I needed was a quest. And what changed the trajectory of my life was that I created one.

All successful entrepreneurs tempt themselves with a goal that currently seems unattainable, something that will take all of their passion to achieve. That's a given. But what you may not know is that human beings are neurologically primed to test their own limits and to eventually succeed. Research shows that the more we push ourselves to discover, try out, and act, the healthier we are likely to be. We want to make magic happen, and when we do, we're pleased with those results.

But there is also a part of us that doesn't even want to succeed.

Did I actually say the weird part out loud? I did. Research unexpectedly reveals that 72 percent of *successful* entrepreneurs suffer from depression or other mental health concerns. Successful CEOs may be depressed at more than double the rate of the public at large. Why? These researchers say it's likely tied to their intrinsic drive, that full-speed-ahead personality that most entrepreneurs share. Once they have reached a certain level of success, they need to find a new plan of action or they risk a mental health crisis.

It's not *having* success that makes us happy. It's the process of *getting* successful that matters.

Let's talk about kids for a moment. Children love to play, and they'll play with anything and in any environment. Kids will jump up on benches and climb trees. They'll grab at any technology within arm's reach. In an amusement park line, they'll try to swing on a rope divider before bringing the whole string of aluminum poles down.

Why do children play? They don't play just to have fun. They play in order to grow and to get better at *doing*.

Outdoor play contributes to the overall brain development of children. The combination of physical activity and creativity increases oxygenation of the brain and ramps up their energy even more. The more that children use their cognitive powers to create and use new play objects, the more their brains create connections between what they know and what they're learning. And more neural connections mean greater brain power.

What's true for kids is also true for adults. What we feed our brains matters. We have to create new quests to attempt if we want to feel good.

There is no greater feeling in life than being challenged, being innovative, being pushed to your limits.

THE CULTURAL RESEARCHER Joseph Campbell tells us we can frame our lives by what he calls the hero's journey. Every human being has their own quest in life, even if they don't recognize it or plan for it. This journey begins with an understanding that we are being beckoned to do something more than what we are doing right now. The quest can be as simple as memorizing our new address or as complex as finding a cure for cancer. But no matter what we want to do, we are beckoned to start a new quest every day.

Think of the time you felt the most alive and fulfilled. It was probably when you were on a quest to expand your horizons in a significant way. Think about important efforts you've made, like aiming for the top of the sales chart, studying for a degree and choosing your first job, or figuring out where to go on your next vacation.

When you start out on a quest, however, you may have the naïve thought that it's going to be easy. *I just have to follow the steps others have laid out before me*, you might say to yourself. But just when you think it's going to be a cakewalk, the obstacles start to occur, and you must be ready for them. Becoming the hero in our story means we must recognize that obstacles are like dragons that need to be slain.

Let's look at the typical steps in a quest from my point of view.

1. Hear the call

My own quest started when I realized that I loved working with people, and that I wanted to make myself successful by making *them* successful.

This is where it all begins—the moment you get that *big idea*. Maybe you've been working a regular job and one day it hits you: *I could make this product much more inexpensively*, or *I've got a killer solution to a client problem*. This is your call to step out of the ordinary world. It's exciting, but also a little terrifying because you don't know what's coming.

What's your call to adventure or next big quest? Sit down with a piece of paper and write it down. And I advise that you make your quest much bigger than you think you can possibly complete, no matter how scary it might feel to name your true goal in writing. Big goals get you to creative thinking on a whole different level from the way smaller goals do. Your brain will start to think of new and innovative ways to reach these magnificent goals you have written down.

2. Cross into reality

My next step was thinking about all of the different pathways I could take to make my clients successful. Sure, I could keep on selling insurance for a living, but I knew that with the same skills I could also look at all of my clients' financial goals. I had to make a list of every possible opportunity so that I could eventually narrow down my quest.

This is where things get real. You're thinking about how to pull together some cash (maybe through savings or investors), create a plan, and build a client list or even a company. You may even be thinking about quitting your current job and leaving behind the safety of a steady paycheck to enter a world that you create for yourself. This is the point where many entrepreneurs face doubt, even if they trust themselves. It's sink or swim, especially if you're learning new skills, meeting new people, and tackling obstacles you didn't even see coming.

Name all of the skills or resources you feel you'll need to learn or acquire to take on your quest. What staff would you need? What types of clients should you target? What technology would you use? Write it all down and do some research on what it would take to acquire all of that. You may not be able to accomplish everything, but you might be able to partner or outsource, or develop a plan for putting your ideas into action eventually. Make a list of what it might take, initially, to develop your ideas further.

3. Overcome the obstacle of you

In *The Art of War*, Sun Tzu says, "Victorious warriors win first and then go to war, while defeated warriors go to war first and then seek to win." He's suggesting that a war is won before it is ever fought. Every entrepreneur goes through trials—it's the grind. Here come the late nights, the rejections, the mistakes, and maybe even a few failed products or partnerships. These are the dragons of your journey, the challenges that test whether you've got what it takes. But this is also how you grow. You start to sharpen your instincts, learn from failure, and build resilience. It can be brutal, but every challenge is pushing you to become a better version of yourself.

For my own quest, I had to look critically at what was blocking my way to success. I wanted a very realistic view of my own limitations. For me, it was the fact that I didn't have a traditional education in wealth management.

Write down all the reasons your plans will never work. Imagine all of the potential obstacles and all the excuses you're likely to make along the way. Trust me, there will be many. Go through all those thoughts and make the list exhaustive. And if you run out of reasons why something won't work, get your friends and family involved. They will definitely tell you millions of reasons it won't work.

4. Find your turning point

You can turn things around and transform your challenges into opportunities. You have to slay your dragon. This is when your business starts gaining momentum—maybe you've landed a big client, launched a successful product, or found a scalable business model. You want to make sure that you're not just an aspiring entrepreneur anymore; you have the ability to evolve into someone who knows the ropes. This is when you start to see yourself and your business potential differently—it can transform from a scrappy idea into something real and impactful.

I had to figure out how to acquire not only a practical education in wealth management, but also the *best* education for achieving my life goals. I knew I had to seek out and listen to business leaders, read the right books, and try out a range of tactics. My goal was to determine the optimal match between my clients and my wealth management products so that I could start delivering on my promise to myself.

To gain wisdom, write down three possible tactics to overcome each of the challenges you named in step 3. Go through each one of these obstacles and think creatively about how you can overcome them. And seek out resources that can help you slay that dragon.

5. Maximize your return

The final step is to start to map your wins. When I realized I was starting to reach some of my goals, I became a different businessperson.

This is where you can reap the rewards of your journey. It's not just about you anymore; it's about what you bring to the world. When you know you've built something that works, the sense of pride that comes with it feels like you've taken a magical elixir that will propel you forward to your next quest.

To know what you'll eventually get out of your effort, you'll have to measure it. What gets measured gets done. Think about how to measure each step toward your goal so that you know you're on track. Write down a specific goal, like having the budget to hire two employees, or tripling your business in three years. Now, let's say you don't triple your business. What happens next? If you grew your business even by a small amount, you still want to measure exactly what you did achieve. Look for alternative ways to assess your success like this along the way.

A quest may, at first, seem almost impossible to accomplish. But it is your birthright to aim for what you want in life. Just by being human, you have the potential to undertake—and overcome—the impossible.

4

Be Like Arnold

"I DON'T WANT to just be in movies, I want to be a *staarrr*!" Imagine Arnold Schwarzenegger saying that line in his signature accent. In fact, you don't have to imagine it if you don't want to—you can watch *Arnold*, a Netflix documentary on Arnold's life and work. It's a fascinating watch.

But if you don't have the time, here's the gist of the story and why it's so important for building your Circle of Vision.

Schwarzenegger was born July 30, 1947, in a little town in Austria called Thal, population 2,240. He worked hard from a very young age, mostly to find solace from his difficult family life and the dyslexia causing him trouble at school. By fourteen, he was competing as a weightlifter; by twenty, he became the youngest-ever Mr. Universe.

Schwarzenegger would go on to win Mr. Olympia seven times. He would become a movie star fronting global blockbusters such as *The Terminator*, *Twins*, *Total Recall*, and even *Kindergarten Cop*, defining a generation of action and comedy heroes in movies that made over $8 billion at the box office. He would meet and marry a scion of American-style royalty, the Kennedy family. He would become a successful real estate businessman. And then, four decades after his first lift in the gym, Schwarzenegger would run for and be elected as governor of California.

Any one of these feats would be impressive. How did he do all these amazing things, many of them in quick succession?

Before I get into my analysis of Schwarzenegger's life choices, let's take a quick look at the bigger picture.

We all make effort in our lives, more or less. And we naturally assume that people who make more effort are the ones more likely to achieve their goals.

But often there's one key factor that we don't account for: the size of the obstacles we face as we try to move ahead in life. Maybe it's because obstacles are harder to enumerate than wins. Maybe it's because many of the obstacles that affect us are hidden. But maybe, if we're lucky, obstacles can help us build resilience.

Back to Schwarzenegger. Remember that difficult family life I mentioned above? He had a seriously abusive childhood, shaped by his father's rage, which affected all of the relationships in his household. It was so abusive that Schwarzenegger didn't attend his father's or brother's funeral when they both passed in the early 1970s. Many people who experience this kind of adverse childhood face significant obstacles as they grow up, but he stood apart from the crowd.

So how did Schwarzenegger even start the process of moving toward success? He had his own Circle of Vision.

Gabriele Oettingen, a German academic and psychologist, has spent her whole career studying what she calls mental contrasting—comparing our dreams with our current reality to identify the obstacles and then find the best way to overcome them. As she explains, anyone can mentally contrast their desired future with the reality that impedes its realization. Mental contrasting helps a person recognize which of their goals are reachable, allowing them to keep clear of unreachable ones.

This doesn't mean that we can't aim high. We can, and we should. But the key to positive mental contrasting is setting clear goals that are incremental. We can't just fixate on the goal itself—we have to imagine the steps to getting there as well.

WITH HIS FAMILY TRAUMA and learning disability, Schwarzenegger had significant obstacles to overcome. In my own life, I may not have faced the same early, critical life challenges as he did, but I certainly had my own. My family split apart when I was young, and even though both my parents were supportive, I was navigating the world on my own early in life. I didn't have a road map.

What Schwarzenegger and I have in common is that we were both focused on our visions. He wanted to be the best in his field, as I did in mine. Both of us kept our eyes on the golden prize at the end of the road, even when the immediate path ahead seemed murky.

You've faced obstacles of your own, I'd wager. And the reason you're reading this book is that you also have your eyes on that prize.

So, how can you be like Schwarzenegger? How can you turn your vision for yourself into reality? Here's my take.

Never be satisfied. From an early age, Schwarzenegger knew he wanted more than the cards he was dealt could offer him. His relentless spirit meant he would never let himself settle into "good enough." In my own career as an entrepreneur, I have made it a priority to be aware of what was on the horizon for myself and my clients. I learned quickly that those who build this awareness are more likely to become the most successful. Keeping your eyes up and forward allows you to take stock of new possibilities.

Set big goals. It wasn't enough just to win; Schwarzenegger wanted to win big. First, he set incremental goals for his bodybuilding work, but once he became satiated with that success, he set an almost impossible goal—to become a global movie star, despite the fact that he hardly spoke English. I also set my own almost impossible goals every year, and by practicing working toward them, I've become better at achieving them. Remember, it's just as easy to set big goals as small ones. Why not set your goals ten times bigger?

Visualize yourself making it happen. Mental contrasting is fully evident in the *Arnold* documentary. In one scene, Schwarzenegger is lying on a small bed in a small town visualizing himself going to the United States. He visualized not only winning Mr. Olympia, but what it would feel like, what he would say, and what he would do next. He reviewed every technique, every move, and every win to continue his incremental steps forward. While I wasn't great at doing this at the beginning of my career, I honed my skills at turning my quests into reality. All entrepreneurs likewise visualize client presentations, a better business, their ideal clients and team, and the freedom they'll gain over time.

Keep track of your progress. At one point in the documentary, in a rudimentary gym, the camera pans to a wall marked by crossed-out lines. Schwarzenegger says that every line represented a rep. His goal was to keep track so that he would know when he was meeting his incremental objectives, and every mark allowed him to see that he was one step closer to his goal. Successful entrepreneurs likewise track the results of their tactics like a religion. They know that if they do more reps, they will continue to improve. In my own work, I've learned that what gets monitored gets done.

Work harder than everyone around you. If there is one thing you can say for Schwarzenegger, it's that he doesn't stop. When he was younger, he was bodybuilding four to six hours a day, attending school for business and English, taking acting lessons, and working a day job. Everyone has the same number of hours in a day; Schwarzenegger showed that it's about how you use them. I may not have put the same number of hours into my work as Schwarzenegger did in the gym, but I learned how to use my time wisely. I also determined that I wanted to work fewer hours rather than more, but to do that I had to get really good at serving my clients' needs, and that takes time. When you work for yourself, it's easy to become complacent and name the competition as your problem. But it's your job to focus on your own efforts and look at how you can better yourself.

Never give up. Despite all of the ups and downs in his career, Schwarzenegger always persevered and kept his eyes on the prize. Every business and every person faces obstacles and challenges, but my experience has taught me that barriers are almost always temporary if you continue to focus on your goals and, in turn, take the time to do all of the small things that need to be checked off to get to those goals. Like Schwarzenegger, you have to keep imagining the end result you want in order to articulate your journey. Doing so means that you're not going to be satisfied with less.

THE CIRCLE OF VISION asks you to answer two very important questions.

1   **How clear is your vision for your future?**
2   **Are you willing to follow your quest to get what you want?**

If you can't answer these questions yet, you won't be able to move forward to the next circle, the Circle of Trust, and make it work for you. Why? Because you have to trust yourself and your vision first before others will trust you, and as we'll discover in the following section, trust is imperative to business success.

Are you still hemming and hawing about what matters to you? Are you concerned about how much energy you're going to have to put into actualizing your vision to get to success? If the answer to these questions is yes, you're going to need to come up with a different vision. Ask yourself how passionate you are about your next steps forward, and if you don't feel like shouting your vision from the rooftops, now is the time to shift your focus. Go back to my two Circle of Vision questions and answer them even more honestly and completely.

Once you're ready to say yes to yourself, turn the page.

CIRCLE TWO

TRUST

THE EFFECT of trust is powerful.

In horseback riding, the arc of the circle shapes what riders and horses expect from one another. Small circles can be more difficult for horses to manage than larger circles, but only physically. Larger circles can be challenging for horses mentally and emotionally, and can cause a horse to lose focus. A trust between the horse and rider is critical to navigating these varying challenges, and the same is true in business: When we build trust with our stakeholders, we know what to expect when things go well and when they don't.

Trust is essential to any business. In wealth management, everyone who walks through my door is looking to assure a secure future. If I can't provide the average family with a safe investment that grows over time, I'm failing at my job, and I'm failing as an entrepreneur. My business wouldn't last a year if I couldn't guarantee my clients' trust.

And trust is essential to *all* businesses, not just wealth management.

For customers, research shows that trust means more frequent purchases. According to a recent study by NielsenIQ, for example, Walmart has built trust with consumers by increasing supply chain transparency and cutting down the cost of packaging among their largest suppliers, like Procter & Gamble. This has not only driven down store prices for consumers, but has also resulted in a 20 percent increase in customer loyalty since the program's start. The same study demonstrated that 46 percent of customers will pay more for goods or services sold by a brand they trust.

For employees, the presence of a high amount of trust in the workplace results in 106 percent more energy and 76 percent more engagement, as well as 50 percent more productivity.

For leaders, trusting their coworkers opens key pathways to professional potential. As Jim Whitehurst, CEO of open-source software maker Red Hat, has said, "I found that being very open about the things I did not know actually had the opposite effect than I would have thought. It helped me build credibility."

These are just a few of the hundreds of ways in which trust is essential for your business's ultimate success.

Building a Circle of Trust enables you to look critically at who you want to draw closer to you, such as the clients you want and the team you need. It allows you to create distance and boundaries where necessary. And it helps you develop the personal and professional traits you must embody if you want to be trusted.

5

Find Your Plumbers

WHEN I bought my first house, I had a revelation.

One early evening, I took a walk through my suburban neighborhood, a newly built oasis outside of the city. I wanted to get a feel for the place and maybe introduce myself to a few of my neighbors. It was nice. The sun was setting behind the homes and their beautifully landscaped lawns, the streetlights were coming on, and it was quiet.

But as I walked, I started to clock something interesting.

Old, beat-up utility vans began to pull up into my neighbor's driveways. I watched as the garage doors opened one after another, and the vans pulled inside. Invariably, however, inside these two- or three-car spaces was a Mercedes, an Audi, or even a Maserati.

An old *Sesame Street* tune started to play in my head: "One of these things is not like the others."

I took a closer look at one of the vans. Smith City Plumbing, it said in large letters on the side, complete with a phone number and website address.

Plumbers. *Huh*, I thought. From the 1990s onward, the number of available plumbers has dwindled as more young adults have been ushered into postsecondary education. But everyone still needs plumbers. Far from a dying profession, it's an in-demand one with the billables to prove it. *Plumbers have a lot of money*, I surmised to myself as I walked. *Do they know what to do with it all?*

As I was a wealth management expert, I decided to find out. I struck up a conversation with one of these plumber neighbors, Frank, introducing myself as a newly arrived member of his community. I found out from Frank that nobody was giving them financial advice.

Within a few months, Frank was not only my client but my personal walking advertisement. He spread the word, and plumber by plumber, I added more clients. I built a specialty around wealth management for plumbers, advising folks like Frank how to invest based on their unique needs.

A lot of entrepreneurs, especially those in financial advising, try to take on every client they can, only to become overwhelmed and under-resourced all too quickly. Early on I learned that not everyone is your client. I became very successful by homing in on the needs of one single type of client. That's how I started to build my Circle of Trust. My new clients trusted me because their friends and colleagues did, and I earned that trust by working hard to understand and fulfill plumbers' investment dreams.

Be everything to somebody, not somebody to everyone.

I'M NOT the only one who feels this way. Warren Buffett, the epitome of wealth managers, has his own circle—the circle of competence. This is the finely honed subject area you choose for a match with your skills and expertise. "The size of that circle is not very important; knowing its boundaries, however, is vital," he has said. In my case, it's not like I knew a lot about plumbing before I approached Frank, but I was willing to learn. As Buffett suggests, his circle is about recognizing and building upon a single passion and developing the competence to meet that passion head-on.

In 2005, Switzerland-based researchers W. Chan Kim and Renée Mauborgne wrote *Blue Ocean Strategy*, an excellent book that suggested that entrepreneurs create a valuable and defensible niche in the ocean of their industry by disrupting the status quo to attract new clients.

It's a great strategy, but what's also true is that there are a lot of fish in that ocean.

When you're getting started in business, it's too easy to get caught in a just-good-enough frame of mind, slightly varying your work from what everyone else in your industry does. The problem with just riffing on what others are doing is that, to a customer-to-be, everybody looks the same. This approach also leads to a keeping-up-with-the-Joneses mentality: You're always looking behind you because someone might overtake you. As your competitors add capacity and innovation, you'll feel compelled to do the same. If you keep trying to be everything to everyone, your value proposition becomes very expensive to maintain. Marketing becomes more expensive and less effective, innovation becomes watered down, team members become confused about their mission and their clients, and your administration becomes complex and full of errors.

And with a just-good-enough mindset, the reality is that your company will focus more on competing on price. Once you start lowering your prices to be competitive, the end is near.

Building a Circle of Trust instead means that the entire game changes.

You don't have to *find* your clients. You can trust that they're already there. Your clients are not lost in the wilderness waiting for you to come up with a unique, disruptive business concept. In fact, as newer research has proven, work is best understood as a lifelong journey where detours and unconventional paths are natural and often valuable.

In other words, forget finding your corner of the blue ocean. Look for a blue pond, fed by a series of rivers and streams. Along those rivers and streams you'll meet up with people you know or want to know. These people make up your own unique entrepreneurial circle of clients, colleagues, and supporters. Taking a diversion down a nearby creek means you can discover people on your own wavelength right now. This little blue pond is your Circle of Trust. Reach financial heights faster and sustain your business long-term by diving into it first.

How can you find your plumbers and build your own Circle of Trust with them?

Stand out to a particular niche market. Show your customers that you're different because you focus on a few key problems that you alone can solve, or solve better than any other business in that market. Define your own space and become known as an expert in it. Southwest Airlines was profitable for forty-seven straight years, and its CEO, Herb Kelleher, was repeatedly voted the best in the airline industry. Part of their success was knowing their niche better than anyone else, and every decision Southwest made was for the benefit of their target customer: the short-haul frequent flyer.

Love the people who make up that market. I mean it. Love your customers in an authentic way. There are two types of wealth management entrepreneurs out there: those who love people and love relationships, and those who focus on giving advice about what kind of investment to buy. Entrepreneurs in the first group succeed 100 percent of the time. The second group is a crapshoot, because investing is a feast-or-famine business (unless you're Warren Buffett himself). Why does the first group succeed? Because when times are challenging, your clients will trust you enough to weather the storm *with* you. Otherwise, they'll be out looking for a new set of options before you have a chance to prove yourself.

Know where your people are and meet them there. Plumbers live in the suburbs outside towns. They need to be close enough to cities to get big gigs, but driving distance to cottage country so that they can maintain their clients' summer homes and preserve those relationships year-round. Pretty soon, plumbers will want to follow their clients' path and buy their own cottage. If you're going to build trust with your clients, you'll have to have an interest in improving outcomes on their terms. You need to get to know their life patterns, their interests, and their barriers to wealth.

Grow with your clients. Building a Circle of Trust means establishing a long-term approach to business. Clients come to me to make important financial decisions, so they need to see me thrive to trust that I'm going to help *them* thrive.

At the end of the day, what clients really want is somebody they can trust and rely on. All that really means is they want entrepreneurs to follow through on what they said they were going to do. Your job is to build out the Circle of Trust so that it's complete, but it should feel like a great big bear hug, not a lasso.

Remember that you're a living emblem of what's possible. Grow your skills and your own potential so that you can take care of others' potential.

6

Solve Obvious Problems

TO PAY his undergraduate tuition at Yale University in 1973, Fred Smith piloted charter flights for companies needing to get computer parts from one state to another as quickly as possible. He had recognized that, in a new age of automation, delivery speed was critical. Without those computer parts, businesses would fail. Smith stepped up and filled that customer need, building the world's largest courier transportation company, FedEx, in the process.

Steve Jobs was out for a jog when his music stopped playing. He asked his team to create a foolproof, skip-free audio device that would allow for a seamless integration between technology and usage. He also thought customers would be happy to pay a premium for an exceptional listening experience, and he was correct. The iPod launched with great success in 2001.

A couple of snowboarders, Daniel Ek and Martin Lorentzon, wanted to sell their equipment online through Amazon's sales platform. But they found it both difficult to use and limited in its ability to present their wares, so they built a platform that could be used by any company and any customer. Shopify addressed Amazon's unmet business-owner needs and launched their highly accessible web system in 2006.

In my own early work as an insurance salesperson, I recognized that my clients often had different needs. Some had the ability to purchase insurance-based investments, and some did not because of product limitations, their age, or a need for more flexible investments. Keeping my ear to the ground, I chose to move my clients into mutual funds and other investment models when the time was right, and I started to specialize in wealth management instead of insurance.

In all of these cases, the companies were successful in creating business opportunities where they didn't exist before. And they have one other key thing in common: They start with the client.

A pretty common business approach is one based on founders creating a product or service, and then trying to find an audience to market that product to. I think that truly great businesses do things the other way round.

In fact, it should be your sole job to solve your potential clients' most obvious problems. That's how they'll know you're worth trusting.

"FOR THIRTY years I've tried to figure out how great leaders do their work exceptionally well," Hal Gregersen, executive director of the MIT Leadership Center, explains when speaking about his research. "I found they were all exceptional at asking better questions—questions that are catalytic, that transform something from what is to what in a very amazing way might be."

As Gregersen tells it, leaders like Smith, Jobs, and the founders of Spotify are experts in what he calls active questioning. They persistently dig into problems, asking themselves and others why problems can't be solved. As a result, they force barriers to creative thinking to fall. In fact, as Gregersen notes, these kinds of leaders spend at least 30 percent of their workday in this questioning process.

How do they tap into solving problems? By starting with being open to accepting what Gregersen calls "passive data." Passive data is the information that *isn't* being collected because it isn't connected to an active strategic goal. For example, walking around and talking to random team members can alert a leader to information that is normally hidden, but incredibly relevant. Anonymously visiting a store could help to improve a company's retail experience. Arranging a meeting of obviously frustrated employees could solve a dispute and lead to innovation. As Gregersen points out, even soliciting negative responses, by asking team members to tell you what they think you don't want to hear, can provide a cascade of new ideas.

In my own work, I set up a really easy way to find problems to solve: I educated my potential clients in active questioning techniques.

Let me dig deep here.

The main challenge for every new business is attracting new and sustainable clients, correct? To grow my wealth management business outside of the plumbing demographic, I had to find more potential clients, people who needed financial advice.

I decided to offer educational sessions on the ins and outs of financial planning. I put together a series of one-hour overviews of topics like Investing 101, Saving for Retirement, and Looking After Your Estate Planning.

I then thought about the kinds of industries that hold staff meetings on a regular basis. I met a friend with a car dealership business over coffee, and he mentioned that I could attend one of their sales meetings. After a successful first session, I started calling other car dealership sales managers and asking if the financial well-being of their staff was important to them. After a series of positive referrals, I did the same presentations at real estate offices.

Every step along the way, I was learning more and more about what each of these demographic groups needed to feel safe in their investment strategy and what advice they needed. In each industry group, I was able to develop a package that worked, based on the questions that they asked me during our education sessions. They needed something tangible to remind them that I put their interests first. They knew that I understood them and was working with them to get what they wanted, so they trusted me.

My really big break landed when I read a news article about a large international company restructuring. They were offering early retirement packages for all employees over the age of fifty-five. Recognizing that these newly freed employees might need financial advice, I called their director of human resources.

"What kind of financial advice are your retirees getting?" I asked.

"Um, nothing," they were embarrassed to admit.

"Listen, I have a six-session program I'm willing to share with your team. I'm happy to help."

I listened to every employee who received that retirement package. Each one left their multinational firm with not only investment advice but knowledge of the amount of income they were going to derive from their investments over the course of their lifetime. The company itself was able to build goodwill by offering this service to their employees.

This experience took my career to its next level, gaining me more clients in one year than I did in my previous five altogether. I learned that the power of really understanding a problem and then providing a customized solution is so much more effective than having a product and then finding a client to sell it to. This is the secret sauce of entrepreneurship.

———

IT'S CRITICAL for entrepreneurs not only to design a solution, but to design the client experience around that solution. Trust is a feeling, and it can only emerge on the basis of an outstanding experience that solves obvious problems.

How do you solve obvious problems? Be an active questioner. Ask questions first, not last. And then listen hard.

Who do you want to help? Decide on your demographic of choice. Let's look at wealth management as an example. One of the biggest recent shifts in investor demographics in the Western world is people moving from being accumulators to de-accumulators. In other words, baby boomers are retiring. They need to shift from putting their money into investments to taking that money out in the most tax-effective manner.

What does that demographic need? Are they motivated by hope or fear? In the case of baby boomer retirees, for example, I get asked the same questions all the time. This is a huge and scary event for most people. They're giving up their income from employment and replacing it with income from their investments, and there are many variables that will affect their success in doing so. What kind of rate of return will they have? What will their cost of living become? How long will they live? Are they planning for their children's needs when they pass away?

What's changing in their lives? In the case of wealth management, asking a client about their family is critical to ensuring that I can take care of obvious needs. A discussion about a retirement party could alert me to their need to eventually support a parent or grandparent. The birth of a new child might trigger a conversation about an education savings account or a trust.

Who and what can serve their needs? As important as listening to our clients is listening to our teams. It's a great idea to understand each of our clients individually, but it's just as important to use active questioning techniques to tap into larger business or industry trends. This way you can create a unique solution for each of your target demographics, because each of these groups has a different set of problems to solve. It can take a village of idea-generators to make that happen.

I've had experiences with companies that uphold their brand values and make you respect them. I've also been at the breaking point with companies that fail in delivering on their promises. I'd never do business with them again. You've probably had these experiences too.

So, which kind of entrepreneur do you want to be? Someone who breaks the intrinsic promise of their business, or someone who solves problems and keeps clients coming back?

7

Decide If You're Pete's Donuts or Tim Hortons

I HAVE A small farm outside of the city. It's my weekend retreat. When I have time off, you can find me grilling in the backyard and opening up a bottle of Brunello for my friends and family. It's quiet up there, the kind of quiet where you can still hear the birds singing and the horses whinnying.

Over the years I've been driving there, I've had the chance to observe two business models in real time. There are two donut shops across the road from each other on the way to the farm. One is called Pete's Donuts, and the other is a Tim Hortons. In Canada, Tim Hortons is the number one donut and coffee shop, a national institution that sells around one hundred times as much coffee as Starbucks in this country.

Pete's Donuts is owned by a guy named Pete. Pete and his daughters get up every morning at 4:30 a.m. to make the donuts for the day. Meanwhile, his wife gets the store ready for opening at 6:30 a.m. Pete and his family serve their customers all day long until closing time, 8 p.m., and they are well-known for their awesome donuts and great coffee. They are also very friendly with their regular customers and have a great reputation.

Pete and his family *are* Pete's Donuts. They encapsulate the whole business. If they were not there to make the donuts, brew the coffee, serve the clients, and take care of every single detail necessary to run the shop, there would be no business. When Pete and his family go on vacation, they have to shut the store down. When Pete retires, the best he can hope for is that one of his children takes over operations.

Across the street is a Tim Hortons owned by a franchisee and run by her hired manager. The franchisee sees her coffee shop as an asset that she can eventually sell to fund her retirement. The business runs itself without any interference from the franchisee, who can take as much time off as she wants, knowing that the business will keep running. Tim Hortons is profitable and a very easy franchise to sell down the line.

Now, let's be clear. Both businesses can be successful, but they require completely different resources, clients, plans, and economic models.

My question to you is this: Are you Pete, or are you the Tim Hortons franchisee?

Does your business need your presence, your input, and your decision-making to operate successfully every day, or can you trust your staff to take care of it in your absence?

Does that business model make sense for your life now, *and* do you trust it to sustain the life you want to have in the future?

In my experience, the bulk of business owners are like Pete. They have a business, but it only operates as if they are alone in that effort, even when they're not. The business would have a very hard time surviving if the owner bowed out. Their clients may love what they do, but the company doesn't have the kind of Circle of Trust that's necessary to keep things going over the long term. Pete isn't setting himself and his family up for the kind of success that I would envision for myself.

ONE OF the most inspirational books I've ever read is *Good to Great* by Jim Collins. Collins's work is based on some exceptional research he conducted over many years. Business school teaches students that successful business strategies are about delivering a *sustainable* competitive advantage—but, as Collins shows in his book, very few companies can actually sustain their success. He examined the performance of 1,435 good companies over a forty-year period and found only eleven companies that proved to be great. These were the only companies in his data set able to survive past that forty-year mark and still make outstanding profits. *Eleven.*

Building a Circle of Trust is part of getting from good to great. To get from creating a good company like Pete's Donuts to a great one like Tim Hortons, you have to recognize three key principles.

Trust yourself. Passion is what drives results. If you're truly passionate about something, you will work hard on it and not let obstacles get in your way. You have to trust yourself to get it right, and to aim higher than you thought possible. You don't have to limit yourself to toiling day after day for a moderate income like Pete; you can move toward business models that have the potential to provide a greater and more sustainable income. And your team has to trust that you, as a leader or coworker, have their backs.

Trust your team. If you're going to be a Tim Hortons kind of person, you're also going to need to trust your team to grow the business just as well as you do. Collins's research identified a number of success factors that are connected to leaders' personalities rather than their financial or organizational prowess. In fact, the kind of company that is able to create sustainable growth is one that focuses on sharing leadership capacity. A leader people trust has professional will, but also personal humility. True leaders are not necessarily those who push their own ideas forward, but those who are able to recognize and support all good ideas within the organization. You have to trust your team members to execute the plan, and to make decisions that matter.

Trust what you're paid to do. Many people are passionate about something, and they can even be the best in the world at it. But if it doesn't drive a financial engine, it's a hobby. What drives the engine for wealth managers, for example, is profit per client. Think about what you get paid to do. As any kind of entrepreneur, you only truly get paid when you create real value for your customers. What the truly great entrepreneurs do is figure out exactly where their time is best spent and focus intently on those activities.

But the most important of these principles is trusting yourself. You have to trust yourself to aim high and get the job done. You, personally, have to get from good to great, and to do that you have to feel great about what you're doing.

Before I discuss how to do just that, let's take a short detour. Have you ever met somebody who seems, well, perfect?

The perfect do walk among us. World-class athletes, Oscar-winning actors, virtuoso musicians. Perfect people even exist in the business world. It's a joy to watch these people at their work because they're just so good at what they do. I've even seen this phenomenon in the service industry—waiters who are so good that it makes you stand in awe. Personally, it's one of my favorite things to observe somebody so obviously practiced to perfection that they just shine.

Did you ever wonder how these stars learned to shine? Let's be clear: Natural talent only goes so far. Some people think that great salespeople were born with the gift of the gab, or musicians were bestowed with some sort of magical genetic talent. The truth of the matter is that most people who are at the top of their game are there because they practiced.

And practiced. And practiced. They continued to refine their craft to become the best in their fields. Now, practice is not just a simple matter of doing the same thing over and over again. Practice builds what is called unconscious competence, namely the ability to build muscle and cognitive memory so that performing at a high level becomes second nature. It's about doing a task and then purposely improving on how you do it every single time. Then if a variable is introduced, like a headwind on a running track, an Olympic runner knows exactly what to do and how to win even though the conditions aren't perfect.

As you know already, I'm a fan of the late Steve Jobs. He became perfect at one thing: convincing people that his ideas had merit. He was known to practice a presentation for eighty hours before he would get up on a stage. He had every nuance of that talk thought out in advance. Every joke, every move, every mannerism was planned and rehearsed, and, like that runner in the headwind, every possible reaction was considered. He was there to create a positive experience, explaining incredibly complex ideas and making them simple. His practice made Jobs one of the great presenters of his generation.

So how does practicing relate to developing self-trust? Self-trust is tied to developing an unconscious competence aligned with your business goal. Once you know you're good at something, you'll trust yourself to succeed every time you use that skill. This is where vision and skill intertwine.

There are three questions you should ask yourself every single time you practice a business skill, or perhaps any skill in life.

What did I think was going to happen? Say you're making a sales presentation. If you don't trust yourself, you may start out doubting that you'll succeed in convincing the client to come on board. You may just hope for the best. If you do trust your own skills, you're more likely to assume you'll stick the landing and get the client to sign the contract.

What really happened? Reflect on the difference between what you wanted to happen and how everything turned out. Did it go the way you predicted? Did it turn out better or worse? Why do you think the sales presentation turned out the way it did?

What would I do differently next time? Decide right away what you could do to make your next sales presentation better. Did you answer every question before it was asked? Did you overcome every objection before it was voiced? Did you really create value in that client's life? And if not, what would you change to make it a better presentation?

Now, let's go back to this chapter's main question. Are you Pete's Donuts or Tim Hortons? You can either build your trust in making the perfect donut, or in creating the most successful business.

It's your choice.

8

Open the Window

TRAVELING THROUGH AFRICA one time on a birthday trip, my wife and I wanted to stay somewhere special. Well in advance, we booked a room with a plunge pool. While I've traveled a lot, I had never been to Africa before and it was supposed to be the trip of a lifetime. The unique amenities of that room, and its breathtaking view of the Indian Ocean, offered both relaxation and the promise of adventure.

But four days prior to our arrival, we got a note from the hotel saying there was a mishap with their reservations. The room that we requested was no longer available.

Needless to say, we were both very disappointed and expressed as much to the hotel's manager. Most companies would have just ignored our dissatisfaction, but this company turned a negative into a positive. The hotel manager rebooked us at a different hotel in the same region that offered a similar type of room to the one we'd requested, but with even more amenities and an even better view. In fact, the room at the new hotel was quite a bit more expensive than our original booking. However, the original hotel manager not only made the arrangements, they also paid the second hotel for our entire stay and even arranged our transportation to the new location at their own expense.

What would have been a grave disappointment turned into one of the best travel experiences I have ever had, thanks to *the* best customer service decision I have ever witnessed. I was very impressed.

Mistakes happen in business. People make errors, systems break down, communication is misunderstood, and just the general messiness of the world interferes with delivering on our promises. When these things happen, to build a Circle of Trust with our customers we always have to do what's right so that our relationships with every one of them will continue to grow.

At every moment, your customers have to understand three things: what you stand for, what you're going to deliver, and how reliable you are.

If they don't get the chance to see your trust values in action, mistrust will take over, and at a much greater rate. Customers might tell one or two people about a very positive experience, but will tell dozens about a negative one.

When you are open to making decisions that put the customer first rather than just following protocol, you create trust by offering consistency and value, things that are truly important to your customers. You also have to maintain that trust by doing exactly what you promised to do, when you promised to do it. In fact, you have to maintain trust even when it costs you a short-term financial loss, just like my own experience proves.

Your clients' problems are your problems, and you're in this together.

THE BASIC challenge for entrepreneurs is that it seems as if no one trusts anyone anymore.

The world is mired in mistrust at all levels—personal, professional, community, national, and global. The rise of online trolling and bullying and the emergence of "fake news" have had a significant negative impact on all of us. This is the case whether or not we believe we are being fed manipulated information by companies, politicians, or other people, even people we know. It affects how we perceive information and even offers of help from other people in our communities.

All of this means that when you're starting out in business with zero customer reputation, you're not at baseline—you're under it. When it comes to trust, you're starting out in the red.

This trend is part of the reason younger generations are demanding complete transparency from the companies that offer them goods and services. When Gen Z and millennial customers rate a brand highly on humanity, for example, they are 15 percent more likely than older generations to spend more money on it and choose it over its competitors. When they rate a brand highly on transparency, the results are even more significant. Gen Z and millennial customers are 30 percent more likely than older generations to spend more on the products of companies they deem to be transparent and 20 percent more likely to choose them over their competitors.

And it's not just younger generations. Year after year, the outdoor clothing retailer Patagonia has shown better performance the more it focuses on transparency efforts. Its sales have quadrupled in the past decade to around $1 billion annually despite the fact that its prices are much higher than its competitors'. Patagonia's customers include not only younger generations but an increasing number of retiring baby boomers looking for quality.

As consumers, we want absolute transparency in terms of what people stand for. We're sick of being told one thing and hearing rumors that there's a whole other truth taking place behind closed doors.

That's not just me being negative; the link between transparency and trust is a big part of the wealth management industry. In twenty out of the twenty-eight countries surveyed a few years ago by the Edelman Trust Barometer, the average trust in institutions is less than 50 percent. What's driving this loss of trust? Trust started dropping during the 2008 global financial crisis and has continued to decline as a result of rapid globalization and change, the effects of which have shifted the status quo in how we make, spend, and save money. Recent scandals involving banks have also fueled public distrust and privacy concerns. These problems of trust are likely to have hindered the true potential of e-commerce and other internet-related activities.

All of this is why transparency is a critical part of building client trust, and therefore critical to your success.

Now, when it comes to authentic connections with our clients, what assurances do they really need?

In my own business, transparency is all about client clarity. My clients approach me when something about their financial situation has been bothering them. They don't know if they're going to have enough to retire. They don't know if they ought to send their kids to private school. They don't know whether they should pay their mortgage down or invest money.

I treat them like adults and tell them how it is. I don't sugarcoat their challenges; for example, I don't hide the possibility that they might have difficulties in the future if they don't make significant changes in how they save and spend. They might not like what I have to say all of the time, but at least they know I'm not hiding something from them.

What does transparency look like, and perhaps more importantly, what does it *feel* like for your clients?

IN MY WORK, transparency starts with me.

Before I go into a client meeting, I list all the questions I would ask if I were talking to a prospective financial advisor. Before I even shake hands with the client, I think through my own interactions with consultants and advisors in all walks of life—what they have offered that made me think, or what they've said that made me wary. I challenge myself to be transparent so that I create a mutual sense of responsibility between myself and the client.

And, of course, one of the questions that's always on the list is: What has been your past experience with other financial advisors? The answer to that question really sets off the conversation. People don't come to my office because they're satisfied with someone else's work.

But competition aside, having this conversation is critical. It's not just about preparing for a sales pitch. When it comes to money, sometimes it is about life and death. I have to present with clarity and ask for it in return to ensure that

I'm serving my clients' best interests. Wealth management is a long-term relationship. I need to be right on the money, so to speak, if we're going to be successful together.

So, where do you start your transparency journey?

Make clarity your number one goal. If you have to fudge the truth in marketing your services, or you're buying followers on social media, you've already lost the game. Be clear and honest, and save everyone time now and down the line.

Anticipate barriers. Make your own list of questions that you would ask someone in your profession. Be real with yourself about what you'd like to know. At the same time, list out any gaps between what you actually offer your clients and what you think they want. Understand that difference.

Be accountable and take ownership. When something goes wrong, or when you don't understand a situation, check yourself first. Be proactively transparent when you're not perfect.

Allow others to be imperfect too. Transparency means that instead of hiding mistakes, everyone owns up to them and moves on. Don't punish your team members for being transparent about their concerns, for example. If you want somebody to lie to you, give them shit for telling you the truth.

The Circle of Trust is about wanting the best for everyone and doing your best to make that happen. Business *is* people, after all. But it's also critical to invest in the future of your business.

This is where the Circle of Focus comes in.

CIRCLE THREE

FOCUS

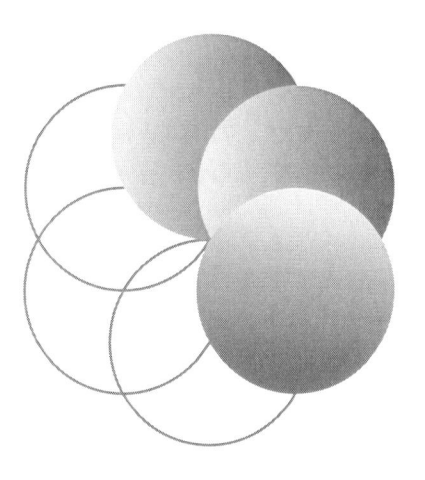

MOST ENTREPRENEURS try to ramp up the complexity of their businesses when what they really should be doing is sharpening their focus.

The Circle of Focus allows your clients and team members to freely choose the right solution for them, eliminating extra work and complications.

Pick up a telescope or microscope and look through it. What you see is inside a circle, because the lens is round, and it's a circle that helps you home in on what matters the most. When you focus a microscope, you're able to focus your attention and notice what's important. Everything in the background fades away.

Taking a focused risk helps entrepreneurs accomplish what they need to do and set aside distractions.

Steve Jobs was forced out as CEO of Apple in 1985, so he founded NeXT and took the helm on the board at the animation studio Pixar instead. In 1996, he sold NeXT to Apple and was rehired as the CEO of the once-flagging company. By the next year, Jobs had stopped development on almost everything on Apple's strategic agenda.

"People think focus means saying yes to the thing you've got to focus on," Jobs said in a talk at the 1997 Apple Worldwide Developers Conference. "But that's not what it means at all. It means saying no to the hundred other good ideas that there are. You have to pick carefully. I'm actually as proud of the things we haven't done as the things I have done. Innovation is saying no to 1,000 things."

In all forms of business, the same adage holds true. When you are able to focus in on what you want to do the most, you'll become the best.

Complexity kills. The focused solution is the best solution.

9

Don't Mess with Success

WHEN I first got into business, I thought I was much smarter than I really was.

As someone who has to evaluate the best and worst financial strategies for my clients, early on I found myself being pitched a lot of new ideas by investment salespeople. A key point about the wealth management industry, as well as many others, is that there is no shortage of products and services. And it's no secret that industry salespeople of all ilks are paid to sell you their specific solutions.

There's nothing wrong with listening to a sales pitch if you recognize who's benefiting: It's primarily the pitcher, not the pitchee. When you're being bombarded with many so-called opportunities, before you know it you may latch onto a trendy solution rather than a realistic one.

Frankly, being subjected to so many options so early in my career landed me in a web of complexity. Even though my heart might have been in the right place, and I thought I was doing what was in the best interest of my client, when I followed the sales-pitch train all I created was a mess for me, and for my clients. Why? For three reasons.

1. It was hard for me to keep up with my clients' needs when I was focused on outside voices.
2. It was even harder to create a great client experience because, over time, it became more difficult to differentiate between possible solutions.
3. I had to hire staff just to help manage the complexity of my business, which increased my overhead.

Luckily, I had an epiphany that changed the game entirely.

One morning, I took a look at my calendar and saw that I had a client coming in for a consultation thirty minutes later. In reviewing their file, I was shocked to see an investment holding I had never heard of. When clients transferred their business to me, they sometimes ported in their older investments, but because I was so mired in the complexity of my business model I realized that neither I nor my team had stopped to evaluate that investment prior to this meeting. I felt embarrassed and felt we let that client down.

I realized I had to change my business completely.

IN TRYING to keep up with their competitors, many entrepreneurs keep messing around with their philosophy, their clients, and their offerings, so much so that they no longer have a hold on what matters: the client.

That's a recipe for failure because you're messing with the key ideas that make your business unique and valuable.

You can't communicate with every client about their personalized needs if you're holding the reins on thousands of different products or services. The more complex your business becomes, the harder it is to provide your clients with an outstanding experience.

When you try to be everything to everybody, it just leads to heartache. As I mentioned earlier, not everybody is your client. You have to try to be everything to *somebody*.

It is far better to have a profitable niche because it allows you to focus on being the best in your field rather than diffusing your time and resources to try to maximize your reach. Build your Circle of Focus by letting go of constant, unneeded changes to your products and services.

Why? Because it's irrelevance, not your competition, that will mess with your potential for success.

And don't just take it from me. Jeff Bezos once said, "If you're competitor-focused, you have to wait until there is a competitor doing something. Being customer-focused allows you to be more pioneering." Terry Leahy had a similar view when he took over at Tesco, the largest British supermarket chain. Leahy, a savvy marketer, had seen Tesco simply copy Sainsbury's, which was the leading supermarket at the time. But following competitors is a bad move—it's slow, it puts you a step behind, and it might even lead you down a path that works for them but not for you.

Research conducted at the Norwegian School of Economics backs Bezos and Leahy up. When a company pushes for new changes just for the sake of it, even when there's no real need, things can get out of hand. Nonstop change can lead to frustration, stress, burnout, and low job satisfaction. It affects not only the employees but also the organization as a whole. Too much change creates chaos, giving bad managers a chance to hide their poor performance in all the confusion, and it makes the company feel unstable—like it's always in a state of disorder. When an organization is more focused on change than on serving customers or getting the job done, effectiveness drops. And client relationships can and will suffer, making your job harder than ever.

Competitive advantage stems from a company's strategic choices and capacity to seize market opportunities. In real terms, however, your focus should be on the word *capacity*, not *opportunities*. What are you doing to ensure that you generate the capacity to support your clients, both right now and a few years down the line?

WHEN I faced the real impact of my choice to offer everything to everyone, I knew I had to focus and stop what I was doing. So I broke my business down into three types of clients.

1. Clients who wanted to accumulate money and were willing to take more risk, and also had a longer time horizon in which to invest
2. Clients who wanted to accumulate money but were a lot more cautious and needed a more balanced approach
3. Clients who needed consistent income from their investments

I developed one solution for each of these key client demographics. Only one. That's it. I knew exactly what they needed to achieve, and I knew they trusted me to deliver the solution. This is not to say I didn't tweak each solution over time, but instead of creating various options I focused in on creating the best investment package possible for each of these groups.

From each solution, I built a total client experience. I developed specific ways to gather information, put together financial plans, and illustrated the benefits to the client. This also included a plan for constant communication with them on how they were doing, as well as an ongoing client review process. (I'll discuss the client experience approach in more detail in chapter 15.)

My plan worked.

Business started to get easier. Administrative errors fell dramatically. Our clients had a great handle on what we were doing for them and how they could plan for the future. Everything became better. Even though it was a niche plan, our growth became exponential.

What can you do in your business?

Strive for simplicity. Remember, be everything to somebody. What are the fundamental deliverables you need to offer? Think like a niche business first and foremost. Even Amazon was a niche business before becoming the behemoth it is today.

Focus all your attention on the things the clients appreciate. And what do clients appreciate? Ask them. What do they remember? What do they feel when they come into your office or leave a meeting? Don't send a survey. Talk to them. Clients will remember the experience, your advice, and the relationship.

Build your clients' trust, always. At the end of the day, what clients really want is a person they like and trust. They value knowing deeply that they can trust you. Be somebody who actually does what they say they're going to do. You can only do that if you focus your offerings, because then it will be easy to remain on top of everything your business accomplishes, every day.

By refocusing my business on these principles, I had the time to ask myself what other opportunities there were in the wealth management space. That's when I was able to begin buying up other dealers—my competitors—and move away from being an advisor.

Not messing with success was the start of a bigger and bolder journey for me. It was the beginning of my journey toward becoming an entrepreneur.

10

Outsource Catching Rabbits

IF YOU want something done right, you have to do it yourself, according to an old adage.

I prefer to follow a different adage: A dog that chases two rabbits goes hungry.

You can't do everything yourself. If you try to pursue too many goals at once, you risk failing to achieve any of them. Just like a dog that can't decide which rabbit to chase and ultimately misses both, people who spread their attention or resources too thin often end up achieving little. By concentrating fully on one objective, you increase your chances of success and avoid the pitfalls of distraction and dilution of effort. It's a lesson in prioritization: Choose what's most important, commit to it, and pursue it wholeheartedly.

And let's be clear: There's always someone who is better than you at something.

There are literally thousands of companies you can hire to take on all sorts of tasks that you don't want to do. These companies devote all their time, energy, and resources to a single task and therefore can usually do a much better job on it than you can, and often at a rate that's cheaper than your time. When you outsource that task, you free up all kinds of time that you can now devote to your most important tasks instead.

There are literally millions of people who can do every task I dislike 100 percent better than I can. The secret is to find those people who absolutely love to do all the things that you dislike doing and build the perfect team.

You can outsource anything. Bookkeeping. Marketing. Client events. Financial planning. Portfolio management. Research. Technology management. You can even outsource social media.

Outsourcing isn't just about your professional life, either. You can outsource mowing your lawn, cleaning your house, buying groceries or clothes, cooking, travel plans.

You can outsource almost everything in your life and spend your time focused on things that allow you to create value. That value can include creating enjoyment in your life so that you're a happier, healthier person ready to offer your best to your clients.

Augment your Circle of Focus by determining what others do better, and outsource to them.

THE PRINCIPLES behind outsourcing apply just as well within your company. Value what your team members do best, and allow them to take the lead where it counts.

I see so many businesspeople micromanaging their team members and telling them how to do their jobs. That makes it even harder to let go and enjoy the freedom of running a business. Whether you're at the top of your organization or somewhere in the middle, it's important to remember that when you're managing people too closely, you really are chasing two rabbits. You're doing your own job, but you're pretty close to doing someone else's as well.

Giving people a lot of leeway to do what they do best results in better outcomes, because in empowering your team, you're giving them permission to feel powerful, and *act* even more powerfully.

"We tend to let our many subsidiaries operate on their own, without our supervising and monitoring them to any degree," Warren Buffett explains. "Most managers use the independence we grant them magnificently, by maintaining an owner-oriented attitude."

Herb Kelleher, the former CEO of Southwest Airlines, agrees.

"If you create an environment where the people truly participate, you don't need control," he says. "They know what needs to be done and they do it. And the more that people will devote themselves to your cause on a voluntary basis, a willing basis, the fewer hierarchies and control mechanisms you need."

Service jobs especially, like those in the wealth management industry, require employees to connect with customers, solve problems on the spot, and adapt quickly to varying needs—skills that demand flexibility, confidence, and a sense of ownership. When you micromanage, employees often feel restricted and stifled, which can lead to frustration and reduced job satisfaction. This in turn impacts their interactions with customers and their ability to deliver on your strategy.

Customer satisfaction relies on genuine personal connections, and micromanagement prevents employees from adding their unique touch, reducing the overall customer experience. Empowered employees who feel trusted are more likely to engage warmly and respond creatively to customer needs, creating memorable experiences.

Ultimately, giving employees the freedom to make decisions and handle situations their way not only builds trust and competence but also leads to higher-quality service, happier customers, and a more productive team.

So, how can you outsource and delegate well?

Start with assessing what you spend time doing. Map your day hour by hour, and consider both weekdays and weekends. All those little tasks add up to massive amounts of your time that you might have spent on more productive activities. Highlight the hours that you've spent working toward your goals or managing your most important tasks.

Narrow your focus even further. List the three tasks that you should be spending your time on. Also list the things you did that prevented you from completing them.

Decide what matters. How do you know when it's time to hire somebody and delegate duties? First, when you find that too much of your time is spent unproductively. Second, when you know that you're not really that good at the task at hand.

Figure out who is better than you at completing tasks outside of your key competencies. Write down the skill set that a person would need to complete those tasks better than you would. Determine if you already know individuals who meet these criteria, at work or at home, and hire them.

Delegate. Really delegate. Be very, very clear on the outcome you want, but let the expert figure out the best way forward to make that happen.

A true flex is realizing that you don't have to do everything to be the boss. Be real with yourself about what you want to do and where you'd like others to take the lead. Then create the conditions in which they'll be successful.

11

Read the Book

FOCUS ISN'T something you can learn once and retain forever. You have to keep checking and sharpening your focus—and adjusting your ability to respond to new ideas and new opportunities. A well-exercised and well-rounded mindset is something you have to develop and practice to keep everything in focus.

Psychologist Carol Dweck has done extensive research on mindsets and has found that a "growth mindset"—basically the belief that abilities and intelligence aren't fixed—can be developed over time with effort and learning. With a fixed mindset, on the other hand, you assume that the world is happening *to* you, and that you ultimately have little to no control over your future.

Having a growth mindset is like rocket fuel for businesspeople because it encourages them to see challenges as chances to learn rather than threats. It also allows them to focus.

Dweck also found that people often have three mistaken ideas about what a growth mindset really means.

"I've always had a growth mindset." A lot of people think having a growth mindset just means being open-minded, flexible, or generally positive—traits they believe they've always had. But that's what Dweck and her colleagues call a *false* growth mindset. The truth is everyone has a mix of both fixed and growth mindsets, and that mix shifts with experience. No one has a 100 percent pure growth mindset, and recognizing that helps us actually grow.

"A growth mindset is all about praising effort." This is a big one. It's not just about cheering people on for trying hard, like giving a high-five to team members in your workplace. Results do matter. Effort that doesn't lead to any learning or progress isn't helpful. The real focus should be on rewarding growth, learning, and improvement. This includes efforts like asking for help, experimenting with new approaches, and turning setbacks into ways to improve. In the end, real progress comes from investing in these deeper processes.

"Just saying you have a growth mindset will make it happen." It's easy for companies to talk about values like growth, empowerment, and innovation. But if they don't back those words up with real actions, those values won't mean anything to employees. That's just magical thinking. Companies with a true growth mindset encourage people to take smart risks, knowing that not every risk will pay off. They reward employees for valuable lessons learned, even if a project didn't meet the original goals. They promote teamwork instead of competition, and they make sure everyone has opportunities to develop and grow. It's not just talk—they reinforce these values with real policies that support growth.

INSTEAD OF just believing you're going to grow your skills and potential, you actually have to do things.

Studies show that just picking up new work skills isn't enough; if you're not growing personally, your performance can actually drop. Feeling connected to a bigger purpose, something that helps you grow as a person, triggers the release of oxytocin, the "feel good" hormone, which supports motivation and well-being.

Simply doing more of what you're already good at brings only small improvements. To see real growth, you have to work on related skills—a concept called nonlinear development. Athletes call this cross-training. For example, runners get better at first by running a few times a week and building up the distance covered. But a seasoned marathoner won't see big gains by just running more. They need to add complementary training like weights, swimming, or cycling to hit the next level.

The same applies to business. If you want to keep growing, you've got to branch out with new skills that go beyond what you already do. This kind of balanced development helps keep your performance strong over the long haul.

Developing cognitive skills, for instance, is like building a stronger foundation for everything else you do. When you work on things like problem-solving, critical thinking, memory, and focus, you're boosting the mental abilities that support all other skills, including those you use at work. This is especially valuable in today's fast-paced world, where things are always changing. Having sharp cognitive skills makes it easier to adapt, learn quickly, and handle complex situations.

For example, if you're improving your memory and focus, you'll find it easier to retain new information and manage tasks without feeling overwhelmed. Strong problem-solving skills help you tackle challenges in new, creative ways rather than just relying on old methods that might not be as effective anymore. Developing these core skills also keeps your mind flexible and open to nonlinear development, so you're ready to learn complementary skills that elevate your performance.

Plus, the confidence boost from strengthening these cognitive abilities can lead to greater motivation and resilience, keeping you energized in your personal growth journey. It's a chain reaction—better cognitive skills lead to better learning and adaptability, which in turn help you grow in your career and beyond.

So, how do I ensure that I'm cultivating a growth mindset and developing my cognitive skills at the same time? I read every business and personal growth book I can get my hands on. My mother's family were all big readers and I got that habit from her very early in life. This is one of the most important habits that have been instilled in me, and I have benefited greatly from it.

Why is it so useful?

First, because I love people and I want to truly understand what makes us all tick. And second, because I know that I don't know everything. I want to be challenged. I want to dig deep and find real answers.

Reading is a simple solution to the problem of how to better understand my clients, my team, and myself. It's a low-stakes way to learn. I can read about someone else's mistakes without having to experience them. Whether it's a biography of a successful entrepreneur, a book on negotiation techniques, or even a novel that gives me insight into empathy and human connection, every book adds another layer to my understanding.

And because of neuroplasticity, these new lessons actually get integrated into my thought processes, changing how I think and act over time. Neuroplasticity is the brain's ability to adapt and rewire itself. Think of it as the brain's version of "muscle memory." When you practice a new skill, your brain strengthens the connections between neurons, creating new pathways that make the task easier over time. This process doesn't just happen when you're young; it can happen at any age. So whether you're learning a new skill, developing a new business, or even just trying to think more positively, neuroplasticity is your brain's way of adjusting and improving, making it more flexible and resilient.

In other words, reading isn't just useful—it's literally changing my brain. I focus by seeking knowledge, reading about new ways of working, and challenging myself to do better by practice. I want to encourage myself to make these new neural connections and become a more flexible thinker so that I can make my business more successful.

And reading helps maintain a positive mindset. By constantly engaging with new material, you're reinforcing the idea that growth is always possible. When business challenges arise, those who read regularly might find they're better equipped to handle them. They're used to seeing things from multiple perspectives, which can lead to better decision-making and problem-solving.

If you want to keep developing your entrepreneurial skills, learn something new every week. How?

Get book recommendations from people you admire. I'm a big fan of a lot of business leaders, but not all of them write books—and some of them, like Steve Jobs, have passed on. But what I can do is read the books that inspired them to do their best work. For example, *The Innovator's Dilemma* by Clayton Christensen was one of Jobs's favorite business books; it explains why leading companies often miss new waves of innovation. Jobs valued its insights, helping Apple avoid common pitfalls.

Read good books, not just the bestsellers. Look for titles that are considered must-reads or that stand the test of time. Jim Collins's *Good to Great* is a perennial bestseller for a reason, just like *The 7 Habits of Highly Effective People* by Stephen Covey. Books that dig deep into real experiences or offer actionable tips are often the most valuable. If a book has rave reviews from leaders and is still popular years after release, that's usually a good sign.

Narrow your focus. Don't just read popular, general books. Look for insight into a specific part of your business journey. Start by thinking about what you're trying to learn—are you interested in strategy, leadership, productivity, or marketing?

Find your experts. Business leaders and popular journalists may write great books, but researchers' work can add a lot of unique value to your reading list. Carol Dweck, for example, started out writing for academic journals alone, but her work is both innovative and easy to follow. Check out business research magazine sites like *Harvard Business Review* and *Stanford Innovation Review* to discover new business findings, and explore delving further into new fields of knowledge.

Read the whole book. So many businesspeople buy a book and read just the first chapter, or leave it on a shelf. Why? Because they aren't actually dedicated to learning. You've got to turn the last page to turn a corner on your learning.

Finally, vet the ideas you read about with your mentor. I love the process of mentorship. For almost twenty years, I had a business coach. I am one of those people who think that every idea they read—and every idea they develop from their reading—is a good one. A coach, or any kind of mentor, brings you back to reality and focus, and they have the ability to help you home in on ideas that are valuable and applicable to your business, not simply those that make a bestseller list. I've since become a mentor myself, and some of my proudest moments are connected to helping people sort through big ideas to find the ones that work for them. Their success is my success.

Your Circle of Focus benefits from your evolving knowledge and the new ideas it will create for your business. The world is full of easily accessible, expert-level information. Don't rely on social media and marketing data for all of your decisions. Find out who knows better than you, and set your sights on what they can inspire in you.

12

Follow the Road to Japan

CARING FOR a bonsai tree is like tending to a miniature world. Every leaf, branch, and root contributes to the living sculpture you're creating. It's a tiny version of something giant. Instead of looking up at this tree, you have to focus inward to see it clearly.

Each day taking care of a bonsai begins with simple observation—examining the soil, touching the leaves, feeling the weight of the pot to sense its need for water. And pruning is an art form here. You have to clip the tree's tiny branches with careful hands, sculpting the bonsai to maintain its miniature proportions and desired shape. Every cut is deliberate, preserving the balance and natural beauty of the tree while encouraging it to thrive in its small world.

Think of a business like a bonsai tree: It's shaped carefully, nurtured, and pruned to grow in a specific way. This is where the Japanese business process of *kaizen* comes in—making small continuous improvements that keep a company healthy and growing just right. It's about making consistent tweaks to processes to achieve big gains over time. Think of it like working smarter, not harder. Instead of overhauling everything at once, *kaizen* is about spotting little things you can improve every day.

Now, *gemba*—in Japanese, the place where real work happens—is the soil and the environment of that bonsai. Spending time at the *gemba*, seeing and understanding the work in action, helps leaders identify where to make those tiny effective tweaks that *kaizen* is all about.

Like shaping a bonsai, managing a business through *gemba* and *kaizen* ensures steady growth, rooted in understanding and deliberate, mindful improvement.

All of these ideas emerged from the work of Taiichi Ohno, the mastermind behind the Toyota Production System. Ohno believed that managers should be on-site, observing the work firsthand to understand how things really work, not just relying on reports or meetings. Ohno taught his managers to watch the actual work processes, talk to the employees who know them best, and look for ways to improve them. But here's the kicker: It's not about finding faults or micromanaging. The goal is to listen, learn, and find opportunities to make things better together. It's a chance to get an unfiltered view of what's going well, what's slowing things down, and what changes could help everyone work smarter.

It's only then, in bringing people together, that *kaizen* techniques can be applied effectively. At Toyota, workers at all levels regularly identify areas where they could boost efficiency, cut waste, or improve quality, even by a tiny bit. Over time, all these small improvements add up, helping the company to be more competitive and innovative and, to this date, the most profitable car company in the world.

Today, *kaizen* has moved beyond the factory floor and is used in businesses, schools, and even personal development practices worldwide. It's all about the idea that you don't need a big fix to get better—just keep focused on improving little by little.

EVERY BUSINESS has the same challenge: hitting the ceiling of complexity. You reach this limit when your business becomes so complex that it couldn't grow if it had to.

Here are some great examples of what I'm talking about.

- General Electric was invested in just about everything—lighting, appliances, jet engines, financial services, you name it. But they got so bogged down juggling not just different products but different types of businesses that it became a huge headache to manage. The complexity just dragged them down, and they couldn't keep up with competitors that were more nimble and focused.

- Back in the day, Sears was the place to shop for everything from clothes to tools to appliances. But they tried to do too much and ended up with a massive, complicated operation that was slow to react when online shopping started taking off. They couldn't keep up with the Amazons of the world because they were stuck in their own tangled web.

- Blockbuster had stores everywhere, but their structure was so rigid that they missed the streaming wave completely. They were focused on late fees, in-store rentals, and following a complex playbook that had worked in the past. But when Netflix came along, Blockbuster couldn't untangle itself from its old way of doing things quickly enough, and it collapsed.

- Yahoo! had their fingers in all sorts of internet pies—search engines, email, news, advertising—but without a clear game plan. Their business became so convoluted that they couldn't compete with the likes of Google and Facebook, which were laser-focused on doing one thing really well.

- Blackberry was super successful with their phones well before others even entered the market. Unfortunately, they had many product lines and security-focused protocols that, while great for certain markets, slowed down their ability to innovate. The company got so wrapped up in its own processes that it couldn't compete with the simplicity and flexibility of Apple and Android.

Businesses grow, and that's a fact. At a certain point, however, the only way you can continue is by making major changes. You have to focus on what your most profitable option is.

Change is hard and that's why many people avoid it at all costs. I've heard many of my peers spout off expressions like "if ain't broke, don't fix it" and "it's good enough for my clients," or the ever-famous "I'm too busy to change." None of these ideas are going to serve your business, because change is inevitable.

But if you can avoid complexity in the first place, you may be on the right path sooner. If you're in the wealth management business or any service profession, start with your client review process. What does a client really want to know? At the heart of their needs, they only want the answers to two questions: Am I going to be okay? Is my family going to be okay?

Sure, your client wants to be able to buy a house, or retire, or send their kids to a great university. But underneath it all, they just want to feel like they're going to be okay. In the case of wealth management, they want to know that they're not throwing their hard-earned money down the toilet.

So, in your client review, why not write a short memo that actually addresses this very real need? Tell your client that they and their family members are going to be okay, and spell out why this is the case. Once the memo is in their file, update it every time you interact. Test out this idea with a few clients and get their reactions. See what they respond to, and make modifications to the text until it is perfect.

THERE IS A Zen-like quality to constantly revisiting what you do, and especially what you are best known for. It's about knowing where to look. Your goal should be to see where and how you can make your client experience that tiny bit better every day through the Circle of Focus.

How does it work? Get back to Japanese basics.

Bonsai. Start with your business itself. Can you prune as you grow? Yes, you can. This doesn't mean you have to work backward or eliminate adding on products or services. The key here is to test and retest new ideas, like I did with my client review. If you have an idea for improving a process, don't wait for a full plan; try a small test right away, even if it's as simple as changing one step.

Gemba. Walk around and talk to everyone on your team. Make it a normal practice, whether you're in charge of everyone or just managing projects. Pick up project files. Look at processes deeply with other people. Make time for conversation.

Kaizen. Turn the smallest possible ideas into action. Encourage team members to jump in with low-risk experiments and get results fast. This way, you can gauge impact without a major investment, and if it works, scale it up from there.

When you start with small actions, you create a culture of momentum in which ideas are constantly being tested, learned from, and refined.

Push yourself to consistently make those small changes so that you have the potential to improve every day. There is no other way forward.

CIRCLE FOUR

VALUE

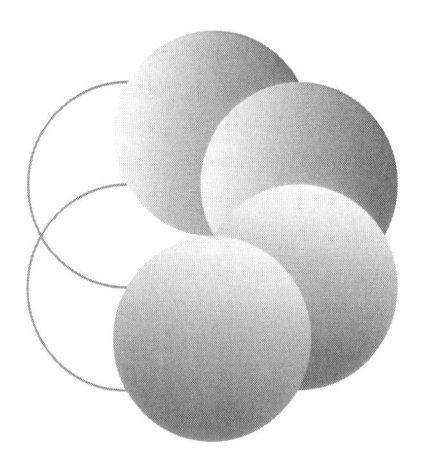

VALUE ISN'T a straight line forward; it's another circle. And the Circle of Value might be the most important circle in this book. You can't make money until you create value—not for yourself, but for other people.

The Circle of Value is like a clock. In business, timing is pivotal. You have to know not only how to build a business, but when to create and follow opportunities. Just as the hands of a clock move with precision, each phase of a business—ideation, growth, and renewal—must align with the right moment to maximize the value you create for your client.

So, how can you create something that others perceive as valuable?

It starts with understanding what people really care about. It's about tapping into their needs and desires, or even solving a pain point they didn't realize they had. To do this, you need to listen closely to your customers, get feedback, and really dig into what makes them tick. And you have to continually recreate value for your clients, colleagues, and community over time.

All of which means that the Circle of Value is not just a circle that goes around and comes around. Just like a clock never stops ticking, the Circle of Value is a continuous process. Businesses that recognize the rhythm of opportunity and challenge, moving with purpose rather than reacting to time constraints, will sustain long-term success. Building a Circle of Value is a test of contact, an indication of awareness, and an understanding of consistent rhythm.

Creating one, therefore, takes both skill and flexibility.

Let's say you invest in training and taking care of your employees. They become more skilled, motivated, and loyal, which enables them to provide better service to your customers. Happy customers stick around, spread the word, and drive more sales, which boosts your revenue. With that extra revenue, you can pay your suppliers on time and maybe even negotiate better deals that keep costs down, which helps your bottom line. And with a stronger business, you can reinvest in your team or improve the customer experience even more.

This creates a self-sustaining loop where meeting one group's needs naturally supports the others. It's about building a cycle that benefits everyone. Meanwhile the system keeps itself running, making sure each piece supports the next, like gears in a well-oiled machine.

13

Map the Little Things

'M LUCKY. At this point in my career, I have the great fortune of being able to travel to some of the most breathtaking places on this planet. As I write this book, I've just returned from a visit to Italy, where I had the pleasure of drinking a glass of Barolo in its home region, and Turkey, where I took a tour over Cappadocia in a hot air balloon with my family.

As I immerse myself in new experiences, I also like my home comforts. Where I can, I'll book myself into the Four Seasons. While their pillows are as plump as the next high-end hotel's, it's their customer service that I rely on.

On a visit to Mexico City, I came down with a sudden illness. Since I wasn't feeling well, my wife called down to room service. She ordered herself a meal but asked them to bring me a ginger ale, as I had an upset stomach. There was nothing more to the night than that; given how I was feeling, we settled in and had an early night.

Waking up the next morning, I felt much better. It was a new day in all respects. I decided to go out and explore the city. As we exited the elevator and walked past the concierge, he reached out to me.

"Mr. Reynolds," he said with a nod. "I hope you're feeling a lot better."

How did he know I wasn't feeling well? I thought to myself.

My wife and I sat down for breakfast. The waiter came over.

"Mr. Reynolds, I understand you're feeling a little under the weather," he said. "May I suggest this remedy that my mother makes for our family?"

He handed me a glass of a concoction I could not name. I drank it and felt even better.

For the rest of my stay, I felt that there was nothing I couldn't handle. I wasn't just a guest at the Four Seasons. It was as if I was surrounded by a loving family who were ready to take care of everything.

Four Seasons understands the client experience. It's their competitive advantage in a very competitive industry. And how do they do that? They pay attention to every small detail, and in doing so make their guests feel extremely special.

I have told this story at least a hundred times to multitudes of people, many of whom now want to visit the Four Seasons hotel in Mexico City just to have this kind of experience.

LIKE YOU, the service experiences I've valued the most are those in which I've felt seen and cared for.

But this chapter isn't about me; it's about the Circle of Value. The kinds of experiences the Four Seasons offers are rare, but they aren't unique. A lot of companies have figured out exactly how to build their Circle of Value—by paying attention to the little things.

Let's look at Chewy, an online pet store founded in 2011 that quickly charmed its way into the hearts of families everywhere. By 2017, this booming pet paradise was so successful that PetSmart scooped it up for an incredible $3 billion. By 2023, Chewy had boosted its active customers' average spending by almost 15 percent.

But Chewy's true secret is its customer-service magic.

Chewy doesn't just deliver pet food; it delivers moments of joy. Handwritten notes in each package show that the founders of Chewy understand that these small, heartfelt gestures have a big impact. They even remember pets' birthdays, sending special cards to pets and their families. And when customers' pets pass away, Chewy sends them paintings of their pets as a way to show they care.

Customers are thrilled to feel this kind of personal connection, especially with an online company. They appreciate the constant reminders that Chewy genuinely cares, not just about pets but about the people who love them.

None of this should be a surprise, but somehow it is. We're so used to companies decreasing their attention to customer service that when we are exposed to this level of client commitment, we're shocked.

Think of the last time you called a bank and tried to actually talk to a person. How long did it take to get through to a human being? Did that person actually listen to you? Were they following a script the whole time, making it harder for you to make your point? Banks can make it very difficult for you to feel like you're not wasting your precious time.

Research shows, however, that companies like Chewy are the ones that are making the most bank these days.

Let's take Deloitte's 2024 personalization report, which demonstrates that nearly three out of four people are more likely to buy from companies that give them a personalized experience—and they'll spend 37 percent more on those brands. The companies that are really good at personalization, meaning they know their customers well, are 47 percent more likely to smash their revenue goals (by about 9.9 percent on average) and 67 percent more likely to see customers buying from them more often.

McKinsey agrees. McKinsey's capabilities report on company performance shows that businesses delivering an outstanding customer experience can outdo their competitors' profits by over 26 percent. Just a small 1 percent edge in customer experience can give a company a 2 percent boost in revenue growth, showing that companies that really know how to connect with their customers see faster revenue growth than their peers. Plus, 71 percent of consumers expect companies to give them personalized experiences, and 76 percent feel frustrated when that doesn't happen.

Here's one example from McKinsey's report. Best Chevrolet, a car dealership in Massachusetts, swears by the idea of "hiring for nice." After sticking with this approach for a few years, they've seen their employees stay longer and customers leave glowing reviews. Their customer satisfaction rating is over 10 points higher than the industry average. In addition, 69 percent of their customers keep coming back for service even five years after buying a car—way above the industry average of 40 percent.

Value starts with the little things.

DAZZLE YOUR clients, delight them, make them feel special, and create processes to do that every single time you interact. What can you do?

Focus on your people, who you hire, and how you train them. While customer commitment is pronounced in luxury brand hotels and dining experiences where an awesome experience makes all the difference, it's clearly relevant in places like Best Chevrolet as well. When you bring on people who are naturally kind, empathetic, and motivated to help, it creates positivity across the entire organization. These are the people who will go the extra mile for a customer, lend a hand to a teammate, and approach every situation with patience and understanding. They don't just check boxes or follow scripts; they truly want to make a positive impact. When you hire people who care, you're ensuring that each interaction, big or small, reflects your company's values, fosters trust, and builds lasting relationships with customers. Elevate the whole team and create a work environment where everyone feels good about what they do.

Make use of your tools. I don't use my customer relationship management systems to constantly bombard clients with valueless emails. Like the Four Seasons and Chewy, I use these systems to track coffee order preferences, birthdays, and meaningful conversations. When I do reach out, it's for a reason that truly benefits the customer—like sharing relevant updates, personalized offers, or useful insights they'll appreciate. This way, each interaction feels meaningful and respects their time. By focusing on delivering real value, I build stronger, more trusting relationships with clients rather than risk the annoyance and indifference that can come from too much irrelevant communication.

Clear obstacles. Give your team the freedom to make each customer happy. When employees have the flexibility to make decisions that personalize and improve each customer's experience, they feel more trusted, engaged, and motivated. This encourages creativity and lets team members bring their own unique touch to every interaction, creating genuine, memorable connections with customers. This freedom also helps them quickly resolve issues on the spot, without needing to follow a strict script or seek constant approval, which ultimately leads to happier customers. For example, Ritz-Carlton gives staff members (including cleaning staff) a kitty of up to $2,000 and encourages them to use that money to resolve customers' issues or requests without requiring prior senior approval.

Remember that word of mouth is everything. People trust recommendations from those they know, so these businesses gain new customers who come in already confident and willing to pay a higher price for something they've heard so many great things about. A strong reputation built through word of mouth also means these companies can focus less on constantly discounting to attract customers and more on delivering quality, knowing their customers will do the talking for them. This cycle of loyalty and referrals keeps these businesses growing steadily, with their premium pricing justified by the quality and trust they've built up over time.

Make your client experience extraordinary every day. Creating a Circle of Value means leaning into your customers' most profound needs, not what they expect routinely.

14

Communicate Constantly

NO RELATIONSHIP EVER broke up because of too much communication.

Communication is like a stone dropped in water—what you say and how you say it creates ripples that extend outward, affecting people far beyond the initial conversation. Just as ripples grow and interact, words and actions influence relationships, shaping trust, understanding, and connection.

Psychologist John Gottman's research into relationships has shed invaluable light on what truly makes them work—or fall apart. With decades of studying couples, Gottman has discovered that successful, long-lasting relationships aren't just built on grand gestures or flawless compatibility; they're built on communication that's open, respectful, and frequent. One of the central ideas that stem from his work is that no one has ever broken up because of too much communication. In fact, the opposite is true: It's a lack of meaningful communication that often causes distance, resentment, and misunderstanding to build up over time.

Gottman emphasizes that healthy communication goes beyond simply talking; it involves sharing openly, listening attentively, and being responsive to each other's needs and emotions. Couples who take the time to truly understand each other's thoughts, concerns, and dreams are better equipped to navigate conflict, feel valued, and build trust. By communicating consistently, they create a bond that grows stronger with each interaction, minimizing the risk of small issues snowballing into bigger, unmanageable problems. In Gottman's view, open communication is like the oxygen of a relationship—it keeps it alive.

Gottman also argues that the same skills that foster a healthy marriage—like active listening, empathy, openness, and conflict resolution—are just as valuable in the workplace. Gottman believes that what works at home works at work because, at their core, all relationships thrive on mutual respect, understanding, and trust. No one feels upset when we treat them with kindness.

For example, Gottman found that "bids" for attention in a marriage—small gestures or comments seeking acknowledgment—play a key role in building emotional closeness. The same concept applies in work settings, where both clients and colleagues make bids to connect or gain support. Just as responding to these bids strengthens a marriage, being responsive to the people you work with builds trust.

Similarly, the way people handle conflict at home—by staying calm, showing empathy, and aiming for a constructive resolution—can improve workplace dynamics as well.

Gottman's findings suggest that treating clients and colleagues with the same patience and open-mindedness we would show a partner or friend can reduce misunderstandings, foster teamwork, and create a supportive culture.

The more we communicate well, the more we're delivering on our Circle of Value.

EVERY BUSINESS should have at least a twenty-four-month communication strategy.

But let's back up for a moment before we dig into that.

In wealth management, the number one complaint from customers about their financial advisors is a lack of communication. What managers hear more often than anything else is "I only hear from my advisor when they want to sell me something."

And yet if you were to ask the average financial advisor, they would say they communicate with their clients on a regular basis.

What's the disconnect? Many advisors send out newsletters and other reports regularly, but these generally have to do with large market trends or what's taking place in the economy as a whole. Most clients don't care about these things. What they want to know is how *they* are doing, not how the market is doing.

Sending out mass emails isn't good enough. The more you can communicate specifically about their particular situation, the more they will pay attention.

In my industry and a lot of others, honesty and thorough preparation are essential.

Mary Erdoes, CEO of JPMorgan Chase's Asset & Wealth Management business, says she asks her team to "tell me the truth, nothing but the truth, so help me God." She emphasizes, "You prep like nothing else."

What is the best way to communicate with most people? With a conversation. In a world that's full of emails, newsletters, and social media, it's wonderful to hear somebody's voice. As well, your entire team should know how often you're going to connect with your clients, and why. By consistently keeping clients informed, you provide them with a deeper understanding of the company and earn valuable insights into their key concerns. This proactive approach not only strengthens relationships but ensures that clients feel valued and confident in their investment.

So, what does that twenty-four-month communication strategy look like? Here's a framework from a wealth management point of view to guide your strategy.

1. Initial Engagement and Relationship Building (Months 1 to 6)

Welcome packet: Send a personalized welcome email or physical packet that includes a detailed overview of your services, important contacts, and an invitation to a kickoff meeting.

Introductory meeting: Conduct a face-to-face meeting to understand client goals, risk tolerance, and preferences, and explain your communication plan.

Quarterly updates: Provide a clear, concise summary of market performance and portfolio status specifically focused on how their investments align with their goals.

Educational content: Connect via webinars or video calls on foundational financial topics to build client knowledge and confidence.

2. Deepening the Relationship (Months 7 to 12)

Quarterly meetings: Conduct in-person review meetings to assess portfolio performance, update clients on market conditions, and discuss any life changes that might impact their financial goals.

Mid-year wealth check: Send a customized report showing progress toward goals with detailed portfolio performance.

Value-added communication: Share personal insights related to their portfolios that make it easier for clients to understand the impact of industry changes on their financial interests.

Client survey: Send a brief survey on client satisfaction and areas for improvement in your service.

3. Reassessing Goals (Months 13 to 18)

Annual planning review meeting: Host a comprehensive meeting to review the portfolio's strategies and adjust any that are no longer aligned with the client's evolving financial situation and objectives.

Goal-tracking update: Send a mid-cycle progress report focusing on how their investments are performing relative to their long-term goals.

Market insights webinar: Host a live webinar to address current market trends and the economic outlook, as well as answer client questions. This reinforces your role as an industry expert.

Client feedback follow-up: Act on the feedback from the client survey, communicating any adjustments made based on their input.

4. Strengthening Trust (Months 19 to 24)

Quarterly updates: Keep clients informed about market and portfolio performance, highlighting any strategic adjustments to their wealth plan and explaining why they were made.

Annual financial planning meeting: Schedule a detailed end-of-year review to assess achievements, reevaluate goals, and set new objectives for the following year.

Value-added service offer: Offer optional sessions on estate planning, tax strategies, or legacy planning to enhance the relationship and demonstrate value beyond portfolio management.

Client appreciation event: Host an exclusive appreciation event to show gratitude, build loyalty, and offer networking opportunities with other clients.

Ongoing Communication Tactics

Monthly market insights email: Share a brief email with current market insights, highlighting how these trends may affect each of your clients' portfolios.

Milestone acknowledgments: Recognize personal milestones like birthdays and anniversaries with a customized message or gift.

Responsive communication policy: Ensure clients get timely responses to any questions or concerns from a dedicated point of contact.

The Circle of Value in a great client experience is about creating a continuous loop of trust, service, and impact. It starts with delivering exceptional quality—products or insights that meet real needs. That value deepens as clients see measurable results, building trust and loyalty. In turn, their success fuels referrals, repeat business, and stronger partnerships, reinforcing the cycle. When businesses consistently add value, they don't just complete a transaction—they create an ongoing relationship where both sides succeed.

15

Provide the Greatest Client Experience

YOU KNOW what Lego is, right? Toy bricks that snap together to become endless possible creations—houses, cars, castles, cities, complete movie sets—all made by the creative builder in everyone, kids and adults alike. With a focus on quality and innovation, Lego has become a global brand, but it's still all about inspiring people to build, explore, and play in their own way. The brand stays true to the valuable concept that what keeps people coming back is the unique feeling of building something from scratch.

But it hasn't always been that way.

A couple of decades ago, Lego lost a significant part of its customer base. Why? Because they focused more on expanding the brand and jumping into new markets instead of actually listening to what their customers—kids and their parents—wanted from playing with Legos. The company assumed that kids, who were more into fast-paced electronic games, wouldn't have the time or patience for the classic plastic bricks anymore. So, Lego started creating what they imagined to be cooler—more intense-looking products that required less time and creativity. But as Lego's style changed, parents began to lose that nostalgic feeling for the original bricks, and stopped buying them as well.

CEO Jørgen Vig Knudstorp needed to make changes. He saw that customers no longer felt connected to Lego and that new product lines weren't the answer. He knew the company needed to dig into the essence of play itself—what kids experience, what they want from it, and how Lego could meet that need. To find out, Lego sent researchers to actually live with families in the US and Germany, where they spent months gathering data, talking to parents and kids, making photo and video diaries, going shopping, and visiting toy stores. They collected a huge amount of information and carefully analyzed it, which led to some big discoveries. One major insight was that kids play to escape their structured lives and to build skills. This disproved the assumption that kids didn't have the patience for Lego—they found that many kids actually wanted the time to commit to it and get good at it.

What can we learn from Lego?

The company chose to go *live with their clients* so that they could dream up the Greatest Client Experience. Lego didn't just listen to their clients; they immersed themselves in how their clients interacted with their products. They learned through following, not through leading.

Paal Smith-Meyer, the head of Lego's new-business group, summed up their findings this way: "You can't force someone to play with the bricks. The research allowed us to make a decision about whom we wanted to reach. It was a decision that grew into a mantra: We're going to start making Legos for people who like Legos for what Legos are."

The takeaway: Ask clients what they actually want. Don't just assume that you know better. Observe before you shift the status quo, not after you've launched a new product or service.

STOP FOR a minute and think about what it's like to go to Walt Disney World in Florida. Even if you haven't been there, or to one of the many Disney resorts around the world, you kind of know what it's like. Sure it's busy, but it's one of the few places on Earth where you can just *feel* the magic. And, like Lego, it's one of the few business entities that has universal appeal.

What does it feel like when you go through the gates for the first time?

What does it feel like to be welcomed?

What does it feel like to be offered not only a service, but the promise of delight?

We expect to be delighted at Disney resorts because, frankly, we pay for that delight. We have high expectations for spending time within the walls of a service business charging us significant fees to enter, and levying additional high prices to eat at their restaurants and take part in extraordinary but safe adventures.

What can we learn from Disney?

Disney makes visits so seamless and fun in comparison to other recreational activities that visitors are enchanted. Disney clients can't wait to see what happens around the next corner. They want to come back, time and time again. Disney embodies the Greatest Client Experience every single day of the year.

Now let's bring these stories together. What do Lego and Disney reveal about business? They offer a Circle of Value around their client experiences.

The Greatest Client Experience is one that clients dream up for themselves, is delightful, and seamlessly fulfills client expectations. It allows clients to see themselves in a unique way: as an explorer, an adventurer, a creator.

Clients are willing to pay for the Greatest Client Experience because it exceeds their dreams and desires.

How do I know this? Because I admired their client experience so much, in the mid-1990s I attended Disney University. I had read a book in which Walt Disney talked about his obsession with creating the happiest place on Earth, and I wanted to see how he did it. I found out that Disney's process mapping team reviews interactions with the client at every step they take through the parks and determines how to make each one a memorable event. I also learned that all the senior executives are required to walk through the parks on kneepads every year to see the facilities from the viewpoint of their primary clients—children. On one such tour, they discovered that the store windows were too high for kids to see the merchandise displays and ended up lowering them all by six inches, at a huge cost to the company. But over the next two years, their sales increased by 40 percent.

So, knowing all of this, let me ask you a deep question: What would you do differently if you charged clients admission to your office?

Chris, that's just ludicrous, you may be thinking. *Of course I'm never going to charge clients to come in for a meeting.*

No, you're not going to charge them a separate fee. But let's be clear: You are billing your clients already. So why should they expect a low-value meeting because it's free, when they can get the Greatest Client Experience instead? They shouldn't. So what should happen?

Your clients' visit to your place of work should be memorable. You want your clients to recommend you to other potential clients. How are they going to remember you?

Your clients should feel good when they come through the door. You want your clients to be honest with you, so they need to feel at ease when they are making important decisions. You also don't want them jumping into plans that don't suit their needs.

Your clients should want to come back. It's important for your clients to feel they can talk to you about changes in their lives and lifestyles so that you can help them succeed. If they feel otherwise, you're not delivering a trustworthy service.

In my office, the Greatest Client Experience looks something like this.

To begin, we hand you a menu. I don't mean a menu of our services—I mean a beverage menu. You mark down your choice—coffee, tea, cappuccino, or something else. We log that choice into our customer relationship management (CRM) system so that the next time you come in, the first thing you'll be asked is "Would you like another cappuccino? Or would you like to see the menu again?" And one of our offices bakes cookies twice a day, so you always smell the fresh cookies on offer when you walk in.

If you're a new client, we may even put up a sign welcoming you to our organization. You'll definitely get a welcome package detailing everything we promise you as a client.

After every meeting, we send out something called the Discovery Letter. Within twenty-four hours of your visit, you'll receive an email from us that sums up what we talked about, what you're looking for, and our next steps. It's simple, but it shows you truly have been heard.

Also, every Monday our team gets together to plan out something special for each client coming in that week. It might be a personalized gift, like an engraved pet collar or a coffee-table book that reflects our last conversation. These little touches add something memorable to every visit.

So, what does your Greatest Client Experience look like?

Don't ask me. Don't ask your colleagues. Ask your clients.

16

Answer Before They Ask

A LONG TIME ago, I came across a magazine article that was titled something like "32 Things You Should Ask a Financial Advisor Before Retaining Them." The article was full of questions people might not think to ask but should—everything from "What's your investment philosophy?" to "How do you get paid?" These are the kinds of things that really matter when you're trusting someone with your money.

After reading it, I thought, *Why not get ahead of these questions?*

My team and I took those thirty-two questions and built a client presentation that answered every single one. We put it all out there, up front. In fact, we went through twenty different iterations in the process of perfecting it. Now, when we sit down with clients, they don't have to worry about holding back or missing a critical question. They get to see who we are, how we operate, and what we value before they even think to ask.

This approach has been a game changer. After we started using this pitch deck, our closing ratio went from 72 percent to 98 percent.

It's a game changer because it has put me, and the rest of my team, in our clients' shoes. We have learned how to home in on their needs by following the golden rule: Treat others like you'd want to be treated.

A solid pitch isn't just a presentation with some facts and figures—it's your story, told in a way that gets people hooked. Think about Steve Jobs. One of his biggest talents was taking complex, sometimes revolutionary ideas and breaking them down into a story that just made sense to everyone. That's what a great deck does.

Our approach shows clients that we're transparent, we've thought through what matters to them, and we're here to make the process as easy and worry-free as possible. Plus, it builds trust from the get-go. They can see we're not just about the basics; we're thinking ahead, answering the tough questions, and making sure they feel confident in their decision.

For me, a deck is about creating a simple, relatable narrative. It's your chance to show people what your business is really about, what problem it solves, and why it matters. When done right, it helps you cut through the noise and capture attention, making it clear why people should care about your business. The best presentations aren't overloaded with details but focus on the core message, the "why" behind what you're doing. Most of all, good presentations build a mutual sense of responsibility between the organization and the client.

They are also there to inspire, spark curiosity, and get your audience leaning in to learn more. It's your story told clearly and powerfully, so whether you're talking to potential clients, new hires, or even investors, they get what you're all about. Creating a pitch deck forces you to boil down your ideas into a simple, compelling message, which can make all the difference in grabbing people's attention and winning them over.

Except when it doesn't.

WITH EVERY successful plan of action, there comes a time when you're going to peak. There's also a time when your efficacy actually starts moving in a negative direction. You'll know when this has happened: You're not closing as many deals, and even before that, you get too many questions. Your prospective clients look confused. And they walk out the door without signing a contract.

That's exactly the time when you've got to look at your pitch deck—and pitch it out.

But before you do, present your deck to yourself. Pretty soon, you'll figure out why your success has levelled off.

To build your Circle of Value, you need a Constant Pitch Deck. My decks never stay the same. They are constantly evolving and getting better. The more I update my deck, the more I'm revitalizing my approach to my work.

As I made the transition from being a financial advisor to an entrepreneur who was buying up competitors, this is the tool that helped keep me grounded. What exactly *was* I selling? Whether I was reaching out to a potential new client at the beginning of my career, or working with a business owner whose company I wanted to buy, or even when I wanted to motivate a team member to achieve a certain result, it was the pitch deck that helped me organize my thoughts. I wasn't focused on what I was selling; I was focused on the person I was selling an idea to. I always put myself in the shoes of my potential audience.

And remember that if you focus intently on your customer, looking at what your competitors are doing remains irrelevant. Complacency is what kills businesses—if you don't keep up with the changing demands of your consumers, your complacency will lead to failure.

So, when you update your client presentations, always ask yourself the following questions.

Why would I do business with myself? Consider the qualities you possess that clients would appreciate, such as reliability, attention to detail, or a deep understanding of your industry. Reflect on your areas of expertise, your communication style, and your commitment to client success. Ask yourself if you deliver on promises consistently and meet or exceed client expectations. Recognize any specialized skills you have that can provide clients with a competitive advantage, such as an extensive network or problem-solving capabilities. When you see yourself through the eyes of a potential client, you know which traits to emphasize in your presentations to build trust and establish credibility.

Where do I create the maximum amount of value for my clients? Pinpoint which of your service offerings provide the greatest impact. This value could come from cost savings, efficiency improvements, or unique insights you provide that help clients make better decisions. Think about how you help clients solve critical issues or achieve their goals faster. You may also add value through personalized service, proactive problem-solving, or staying ahead of industry trends. Assess which of your services consistently generate positive feedback or results, and focus on these when presenting to clients.

What problems am I actually solving, and which clients am I doing the best for? Define the types of challenges your services address, such as improving efficiency, reducing costs, or enhancing client experiences. Think about the clients who have seen the greatest improvements due to your services and analyze why you were able to make such a strong impact. This reflection may reveal specific client industries, business sizes, or particular needs that align well with your strengths. By identifying these, you can better focus your efforts on targeting similar clients and refining your solutions to meet their unique demands. Additionally, communicating these successes in presentations gives prospective clients confidence in your ability to address their own needs effectively. This process not only helps with client acquisition but also allows you to continually refine and improve your offerings based on real success stories.

If I were my client, what would I need to know to make a final decision to do business with me? Prospective clients may want to know about your qualifications, past successes, the specific results they can expect, and how you compare to competitors. This may include testimonials, case studies, and examples of measurable outcomes. They'll also want to understand your process, including timelines, costs, and the expected level of client involvement. Providing this information clearly can address any hesitations clients might have and instill confidence in your ability to deliver.

In delivering your Circle of Value, you have to emphasize your unique selling points, such as specialized expertise or innovative approaches that differentiate you from others.

Providing detailed, relevant information demonstrates that you understand client needs, have the experience to meet them, and are transparent about what you offer.

CIRCLE FIVE

RELATIONSHIPS

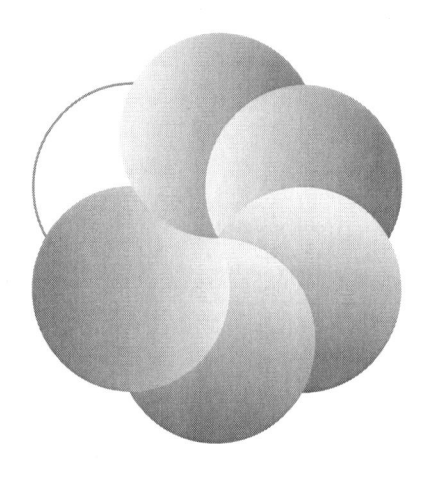

THE SYMBOL of most people's most important relationship is a circle—a wedding ring, representing commitment and unity. But the Circle of Relationships extends far beyond marriage. A family circle shapes our values and gives us a sense of belonging. A circle of friends provides camaraderie, encouragement, and shared experiences that enrich our lives. In business, a circle of partnerships and networks determines opportunities and long-term success.

When we invest in these circles with intention, we create a dynamic network where support, opportunity, and growth enhance each other, demonstrating the power of human connection.

As discussed earlier, business relationships begin with excellent communication, but there is more to it than that. Your clients, team members, and suppliers require you to have emotional maturity and other relationship skills to understand their unspoken needs.

Emotional maturity in business isn't just a "nice to have"—it's what helps keep everything running smoothly. Imagine trying to juggle the expectations of employees, customers, investors, and partners without the ability to keep your cool. It would be chaos! When leaders and team members have emotional maturity, they can manage stress, avoid knee-jerk reactions, and keep things positive and productive.

Strong relationships are built on consistency, trust, and reciprocity. They expand when nurtured, contract when neglected, and hold the power to lead to both personal and professional fulfillment.

You need to build support systems for yourself as much as you need to build them for your trusted circle of allies. Supported, mature leaders are less likely to burn themselves out—or others—because they know how to set boundaries and balance their emotions. And when you're at your best, you bring out the best in everyone around you.

No matter what, the Circle of Relationships in your business starts and ends with you.

Lead generously. Listen carefully. And respond with commitment.

17

Create Deep Relationships

IMAGINE WALKING into a showroom to buy a car and having a salesperson show you a top-of-the-line model. They explain all of the car's great features, raving about how fast it can go, the great handling, the smooth ride.

"Yes, let's do it," you say and shake hands. You set up a payment agreement for the car and await your new ride.

A few weeks later, it's time to pick it up. You're excited. The salesperson hands over the keys and you get behind the wheel to start the car.

Nothing happens.

"Why isn't the car working?" you ask.

"Well, you paid for the car, but you never asked for an engine," the salesperson says, shrugging. "If you start on our new engine plan at an extra $500 a month, we'll send you the engine pieces as they come in. Then you can put it together yourself. Or we can do that for you, for a fee, of course."

You sign a new contract and wait for the parts. But when the car and engine are fully paid off and finally assembled a few years later, the salesperson comes back to you with your contract.

"Your car is perfect. We're going to take it back to the showroom now."

"What?" you say in shock.

"Oh, unless you want to keep it, that is. Your monthly fee to rent it will be $1,500 a month."

This isn't just a strange fable. It's a reality in negotiating tech solutions in the wealth management business. Because we need to connect people, statistics, and products efficiently and at scale, wealth management technology can cost millions of dollars. And because of the profit potential for vendors, we frequently get pitched on the value of new tech. Tech companies make wild promises about all the things their technology will do and all the problems it will solve.

But many of these promises fall short, and it's not because the software isn't good. It's because a lot is left unsaid.

The new car fable is an exact equivalent of our experience with a particular software vendor. They promised a whole lot of features and functionality, but nothing worked until we spent a great deal of time and money on what amounted to investing in their business. Once the product was working to our specifications, they wanted to charge us a high monthly fee, even though we had paid for the build.

Now, I'll take some of the blame for being far too trusting and not demanding documentation and a proof of concept up front. But the outcome of this debacle was a huge debate with no clear winners. The tech vendor wasn't committed to making it right. We ended up canceling the entire agreement at a great cost to us, and a huge hit to the vendor's future business and its brand.

There is nothing worse than the feeling that you're getting ripped off, that you're not being treated with respect or getting what you paid for. I've had this kind of experience countless times throughout my life. There was always something I could sense going wrong, and yet my professionalism has, at times, stood in the way of my gut instinct. I assumed that I had strong relationships with my vendors and that we'd solve problems together, when in reality the opposite was true. When this has happened to me, the feelings have sometimes resulted in irrational decisions.

IT TURNS out that we're all wired to spot fake relationships—and it stresses us out.

Researchers have long known that when we sense someone is being inauthentic, our brains react as if we're facing a threat. Our heart rate actually goes up, and we start feeling uncomfortable even if we can't put our finger on why. It's like our bodies just *know* something is off, and it puts us on high alert.

On the flip side, authenticity has the opposite effect. When someone is genuine, even if they're showing their flaws or admitting they don't have all the answers, it makes us feel more relaxed. We're able to let our guard down because we can trust that what we see is what we'll get. And trust is what helps build real connections.

In 1995, Herb Kelleher and his Southwest Airlines management team were hammering out a new contract with the pilots' union. The deal on the table was a five-year wage freeze, but in exchange, pilots would get stock options they could cash in after ten years. The pilots proposed a certain number of options, but Kelleher actually suggested they ask for *more*. He knew that if they didn't bump up those options, they wouldn't get as much out of the deal in the long run. So, with his encouragement, they upped the number.

Then, after everything was agreed upon, Kelleher went back to the pilots and said, "Hey, if you're freezing your wages, I'm doing the same." He froze his salary, too, showing them that he was in it with them for the long haul. It was classic Kelleher—making sure the deal was fair and that he was right there alongside his team.

But Kelleher wasn't just a nice guy. He was a strategic one.

Creating authentic goodwill by getting right down to the bottom line meant that his team would be able to offer their best to the company's clientele.

Instead of heart rates going up, they went down.

The same patterns are true for clients. When a deal isn't right for them, they'll innately sense something is off, even if they don't know why. They won't be willing to make a deal if they're waiting for the other shoe to drop.

Being authentic—showing up as yourself, vulnerabilities and all—is one of the best ways to put people at ease. When people feel they're dealing with someone real, they can relax, listen better, and respond more openly. It's a natural human reaction: We're drawn to people who don't seem to be hiding something. Authenticity isn't just nice; it's a way to create comfort and a genuine connection that leads to the best outcomes for everyone.

WHY IS all of this important? Well, it's important to me because I love the wealth management business.

The reason I love it is that it's multidimensional. When I was an advisor, my primary role was to address clients' financial needs or problems and guide them to the right decisions for their finances over a long period of time. But to do this the right way, I needed to develop deep and meaningful relationships with my clients. I needed to know everything about them, not just their immediate objectives. I needed to know who their kids were, when and where they liked to go on vacation, if they were taking care of their elders, and what they wanted for their family in the future.

Helping clients is not just a business opportunity; it's an awesome responsibility. But over time, and in many business settings, many of us forget about our responsibility to people, and who those people are.

If we're not competent in building deep relationships and don't keep showing up authentically, we'll never be successful. If we want to build real commitment with our clients and our team, we have to offer authenticity, kindness, respect, trust, and transparency at every turn. It's not enough to fulfill needs—we have to dive deep to build a sustainable Circle of Relationships.

Businesspeople who care about things bigger than themselves—like fairness, equality, and loyalty—build a foundation of trust and respect that benefits everyone around them. These aren't just woo-woo ideas; they're values that are essential for keeping all stakeholders strong, loyal, and committed.

In my own work, I've come to learn that when someone is genuinely appreciative and caring toward others, it shows.

Gratitude and goodwill push them to act in ways that reflect those bigger values, like honesty and equality, that people can see and feel. When approached this way, a business's clients are more likely to listen and notice where they're deriving a benefit. And when a business leader embodies these values, people feel appreciated and respected, which strengthens connections across the board.

Building deep relationships creates a positive, committed culture where people know they're working with someone real, someone who has their back and stands for something beyond just business.

So, where do you start?

Be open. People want to work with someone who's real, not just a professional persona. Begin by being open and showing a bit of who you are—share your values, your goals, and even your quirks. This lets others see that you're not just in it for the business transaction but for something more profound.

Next, listen. It sounds simple, but most people just wait for their turn to talk. Really tune in to what the other person is saying, ask follow-up questions, and show you're interested in what matters to them. Remember things about their lives and bring them up later—it shows you care and aren't just going through the motions.

Follow through on your promises, even the little ones. If you said you'd send an email or check in on a project, make sure you do it. Consistency builds trust, and trust is the foundation of any deep relationship. When people know they can count on you, they'll feel safer and more willing to open up.

Be there when times get tough. Supporting someone through a challenge is the ultimate trust-builder. It shows you're invested in them as a person, not just as a business partner. When you approach relationships this way, you create a culture where people feel connected and committed, which goes beyond just business.

18

Don't Manage People

HORST SCHULZE, cofounder of the estimable Ritz-Carlton hotel chain, recommends giving control to employees every single day.

"Orders and directions don't work," he has said, adding that a better approach is saying, "Hey, we want to improve that, and in fact, you can improve it. *You.*"

Leadership isn't just about giving orders or making sure every detail's done the way you imagine it. It's about balancing that constant pull to control with the need to let your team breathe and grow.

Top client-centered leaders recognize the very common urge to control others—even when it feels easier to let go of the reins. In the heat of daily pressures, it's tempting to jump in with "do it this way" or "just follow these steps." But every time you do, you chip away at your team's sense of ownership, purpose, and motivation. Eventually, they stop thinking for themselves, stop pushing for more, and start just going through the motions.

Researchers looked at feedback from 2,852 team members that rated 559 different leaders on 49 different behaviors. The top behaviors that helped people make real changes all started with one thing: inspiration. Inspiring leaders know how to make a real emotional connection with their teams. They don't use fear or pressure; instead, they spark a sense of genuine desire and motivation in others.

When you let your team find their way and make decisions, you give them space to use their minds and learn from their own mistakes. And that's where they find meaning in their work and the confidence to take on bigger challenges. Yes, stepping back is harder, and it means you won't always get the exact result you pictured. But in the long run, you'll end up with a team that feels empowered and genuinely invested in their work.

You can't manage people—you can only manage tactics and rewards. That's why it's critical to lead by inspiration rather than intimidation. Excellent entrepreneurial leaders try to focus on helping people be their best, clearing obstacles, and giving them the freedom to make the customer happy.

That's what leadership is all about—not just getting things done but building people up, creating a culture where purpose thrives, and giving your team the trust and freedom they need to grow. When it comes to the Circle of Relationships between employees and leaders, if our boss looks at us and sees our best qualities—the potential, the strengths, the stuff we sometimes don't even see in ourselves—it lights a fire.

When someone believes in us like that, it's almost contagious. We start wanting to live up to that positive view, to become the person they think we can be.

Think about why you chose your spouse, or why you adore your grandparents. What exactly is it about the relationship that matters to you? Most of all, these relationships usually offer unconditional support. Truly unconditional. When things get tough, these are the people who have your back. They believe in you because they know you're good enough just the way you are.

As someone who is aiming to run their own business, you will need to provide that kind of support in your Circle of Relationships.

LOOKING BACK to working on my father's farm when I was a kid, I was given the benefit of the doubt not only by my father, but by other more senior hands. When it comes to managing the needs of thoroughbreds, there's a lot at stake, so experience is important. But a farm is also an ever-changing landscape. The horses themselves are growing and learning. So at any moment of the day, inexperienced workers might be faced with the care of an unhappy and uncontrollable animal—one that is also worth a lot of money.

The longer I worked at the track, the more often the tycoon cowboy would ask me to pitch in when he came to visit. He knew that I looked up to him. So when he gave me the chance to help him with his steeds, I would drop everything. I realized he had confidence in me, so I felt more willing to step out of my comfort zone and aim higher. By the end of my time at the track, I was the one he'd call in first.

From that experience, I learned that the more someone recognizes another person's potential, the more that person wants to fulfill it. When leaders do this, it's not just motivating; it's transformative. It instills an elevated self-belief that pushes people to improve, grow, and take on new challenges.

It's this aspect of the Circle of Relationships that makes us better, both in our work and in ourselves. It's not about giving empty compliments or ignoring mistakes. I genuinely see the best in people and recognize what they bring to the table. I see my team members not just as they are but as they could be in the future.

This is a cycle that keeps building, and the easiest way to make it happen is to start with a feedback loop.

A feedback loop could look like adding a new product feature suggested by a team member, who then collects customer reactions or data on how well it's working. That feedback helps the team decide if they should keep improving the feature, make changes, or go in a different direction entirely. The loop keeps repeating: action, feedback, adjustment, and so on, which helps things improve over time.

There are two main types of feedback loops:

Positive feedback loop: If something is going well and you keep reinforcing it with positive feedback, the impact keeps growing. In a social media context, for instance, more likes and shares bring more visibility, which attracts even more likes and shares.

Negative feedback loop: If something starts to get off track, a negative feedback loop corrects it. For example, if a project starts to fall behind schedule, feedback on progress might lead to adjustments in pace or resources to get back on track.

Simply try something that a team member suggests. Start small, experiment, get feedback, refine, and do it again. Continue to look at each aspect of your business, and remember that your team must learn fast and adjust quickly if new ideas are not working.

Why does this work so well? Because it attends to ideas both good and bad without value judgment. There are times when senior team members fall in love with their ideas, even when they are not viable. There are other times when junior team members don't get the attention they deserve. With a feedback loop practice in place, there's neutrality in testing out ideas, giving everyone support while also ensuring that everyone learns strategically.

What else can you do to build your Circle of Relationships within your home team?

Get the best people. To quote Howard Schultz, the founder and former CEO of Starbucks: "We are not in the coffee business serving people, but in the people business serving coffee." Always hire the best team, not the cheapest one. You can never do it alone, so you need a team that buys into your vision and will help you scale. It's better to hire motivated people who clearly understand the results you want.

Build momentum. Complacency stops a company from innovating, driving forward, and trying to grow. To keep momentum going, your whole team should be focused on what I call the little wins: weekly objectives that are set by the team to take steps toward the ultimate goal. For example, calling five existing clients per week just to ask how they're doing provides an opportunity to learn and bring ideas back to the team.

Continue to refine. Keep learning about what makes your Circle of Relationships happy, and refine your processes accordingly. This is a journey, never a destination.

Always measure. If you want something done that's really important, figure out how to measure it, and make both that process and the result perfectly clear to your team.

Harness the power of celebration more often than you've ever considered before. People often focus on the bad aspects of something and ignore the good, and it's easy to fall into the trap of constant negative feedback. Celebrate every little win, and let your team know they're valued.

19

Keep Raving Fans, Drop the Rest

THERE ARE three types of clients in this world. The first is what I call the raving fan.

You love them, and they love you. You can't wait to see them, and they can't wait to see you. When you see them in your calendar, you'll likely have a big smile on your face. You'll probably spend three-quarters of your meeting time catching up and only a quarter on actual business. They listen to advice. They follow the program. They love the concept of financial planning and sticking to a plan. They're low maintenance from a service point of view. And, even better, they send a steady stream of referrals your way because they love your business so much. If you're able to spend time with a raving fan every day, it might feel like you don't even need to get paid.

The second type is the BAU (business as usual) client.

BAUs are the clients who just pay the bills. They're steady. They're good people. There's nothing wrong with them, but they're just not deeply interested in doing anything more than filling in the blanks. They're comfortable paying for services, but there's not much more to the relationship than that. They need advice, but they'll only call your office when you call them first.

The third type of client is your unprofitable relationships, split into two subtypes.

One group is financially unprofitable—either they don't have enough money or you can't solve their problems. They take more time to help than any other client, so they're a drain on your time and your team. The other group is emotionally unprofitable. They question everything. They generally don't follow your advice. They can be rude. These are the clients who you dislike, and who dislike you.

Now, there is a school of thought around client segmentation that suggests you should spend the most time on the clients who make you the most money. I completely understand this point of view, but I find that it's very difficult to pull off in practical terms. The whole idea of having A-list, B-list, and C-list clients, and then providing each group a specific level of service, is very difficult for a small team to do effectively.

Another school of thought argues that you should add a junior associate to look after your unprofitable relationships. This I never understood because I'm not sure why a business would want to increase their overhead to look after their least profitable clients.

But let's get back to raving fans for a moment. The idea is both an old one and a new one.

Ludwig Wittgenstein was an Austrian-British philosopher who's considered one of the most influential thinkers of the twentieth century. His story is a great example of the power of raving fans. He wasn't popular in the conventional sense—he didn't write a bestseller in his lifetime. But he had a core group of die-hard believers like Bertrand Russell and John Maynard Keynes, both brilliant and influential figures themselves, who paid his bills. These guys weren't just interested—they believed Wittgenstein was onto something profound, even if it was complex and eccentric. They became his mouthpieces and helped spread his ideas into academic and philosophical circles, giving his work longevity and influence.

On the other hand, Kevin Kelly, the American writer, futurist, and cofounder of *Wired* magazine, introduced his "1,000 True Fans" theory only fifteen years ago. The theory is that small business owners can make a sustainable living by focusing on building a relatively small but dedicated fan base rather than trying to achieve mass appeal. Kelly based this idea on a simple calculation. If each of 1,000 true fans spends $100 per year on someone's work, that amounts to $100,000 in revenue. For many up-and-coming entrepreneurs, that's enough to support themselves and start building business momentum.

Throughout history, having a handful of intensely devoted followers has been way more valuable for a business than a massive group of casual admirers. Think of it this way: If you're providing a product or service, the people who are mildly interested might like your work, but they aren't changing their lives for it. They're not telling their friends, buying everything you produce, or championing your ideas everywhere they go.

In contrast, those few passionate fans will go to extraordinary lengths for you. They'll buy into every deal, attend every workshop, and spread the word to anyone who will listen. They're the ones who really amplify your impact. They're like your personal cheerleaders, each acting as a multiplier for your work and generating that Circle of Value ripple effect, which reaches much further than a BAU ever could.

And here's the kicker: People who don't like your work have zero effect on your success. There's no such thing as "anti-support" or "anti-purchase." If someone hates your service or product, they just don't engage. So their lack of support is irrelevant. It's the loyal fans who give you that sustained lift and influence.

KNOWING ALL of this, where should you spend your time when it comes to your own Circle of Relationships?

Let's start at the bottom and work our way up.

Unprofitable relationship clients. Every six months, bundle these clients off and get rid of them. If you're in a service business like wealth management, accountancy, or even wholesaling, you may be able to sell those clients to a firm willing to put up with them. Think about buffaloes crossing the plain: They'll only travel as fast as the slowest buffalo. As predators begin to take out the weak ones, the herd speeds up and that's how they make it to the next watering hole. But if the weakest didn't get picked off, the whole pack would be dragged down.

BAU clients. Identify four or five per quarter and try to move them up to the raving fan category. How do you do this? By spending more time with them to better understand their situation and how you can be of service to them. Think of these clients as like birds waiting in the trees. If you feed them and put out a birdbath, they may come close and even stay there. If you do something drastic, you'll risk them flying away.

Raving fans. Your best strategy can be described in one word: love. You want to love your raving fans and spend as much time with them as you can. You want to call them on a regular basis and take them out to dinner. Engaging with a raving fan deepens the relationship and improves your bottom line. This is where you should spend your time.

20

Sustain Yourself

BURNOUT IS a real thing.

I come from a long line of workaholics. My dad was a workaholic, and so was his dad. On my mother's side my grandfather was a workaholic. My brother was a workaholic. The talk around the dinner table was about how early everyone got up, how busy everyone was, how much in demand they were, how late they had to work—and how tired they were. They used to say all this with pride in their voice. Every member of my family was defined by how busy they could say they were.

As I grew up, I met many, many other people just like them. People who talked about how they could never take holidays because the business needed them for every decision. Consistently it was these people who got sick or burned out, and by the end of their working career, they come to wish they had spent more time doing anything else but work.

Psychologist Sabine Sonnentag's research on occupational stress, conducted over decades, highlights a powerful yet simple truth: Stepping away from work is crucial for staying productive.

Sonnentag found that people who don't really "switch off" from their jobs end up feeling more burned out. When work is constantly on your mind, even after hours, it eats into your energy reserves and leaves you feeling drained. It's like trying to drive a car without ever stopping to fill up the tank—you're bound to run out of gas sooner or later.

On the flip side, Sonnentag explains, those who make an effort to fully detach—whether by spending time with family, pursuing hobbies, or just relaxing—come back feeling recharged and ready to tackle their tasks. This mental break helps people recover from daily job stress and makes them more enthusiastic about their work when they return. They're not only less likely to feel exhausted, they're also more focused, motivated, and productive on the job.

What's even more interesting is that recovery and engagement feed off each other. When you're well rested, you're more likely to be deeply engaged when you're working. And the more engaged you are, the better your performance and satisfaction, which also helps you feel more energized. It's a positive cycle that makes the work experience better overall, just by taking a little time to truly unplug.

You need time off for sustainable high performance, so your Circle of Relationships has to include your relationship with yourself.

For me, living in Miami through the coldest months of the year is how I regenerate, because I know that great ideas come to a rested mind. In fact, without self-sustaining behaviors like taking vacations, you could actually be hurting yourself. Constantly working—even during weekends, holidays, or late at night—often backfires because it drains the natural drive and enthusiasm people feel for their work.

Here's why: Research shows that when people end up working during their "off time," it messes with their motivation by sparking thoughts of what they're missing out on. Instead of being absorbed in their tasks, they find themselves thinking things like "I could be relaxing with my family" or "I could be outside enjoying this nice weather."

These thoughts are called "upward counterfactuals," meaning people imagining better alternatives to their current situation. The more they think about what they *could* be doing instead of working, the less happy and motivated they feel about the work itself.

Eventually, the constant push to work during downtime makes people feel like work is an obstacle rather than something they're excited to dive into. Despite this, many people spend time at the office even during their "time off." When they come back to the office for real, out of an eight-hour day they'll work about three productive hours. Personally, I believe this is even worse than daydreaming about what else they could be doing.

Whether you're taking a few weeks or a few months off per year, you need to be able to decompress from work fully. Your relationship with yourself needs to come first if you're going to serve your business effectively.

Yes, you can simply take time off. But here are some suggestions that will help you help yourself.

Make the most of every evening. The research I've noted above shows that doing things you enjoy after work makes you feel better and more motivated the next day. Physical activities and truly stepping away from work thoughts are especially helpful. So, make it a priority to find something each evening that brings you joy and lets you relax. Personally, I'm always ready to toss steaks on the grill and relax with my family, especially if the weather is nice.

Take mini-breaks during the day. Short breaks throughout your workday are key to keeping up your energy. Little pauses to stretch, walk, or do something refreshing are actually more helpful than squeezing in extra work tasks. These quick resets make a big difference. I love finding time to connect with my favorite people to regenerate.

Take more short vacations instead of fewer long ones. Instead of saving up time and money for one giant trek around the world, try to schedule mini-vacations more often. A colleague of mine takes short vacations every single month, even if it's just a three-day getaway, just to get a change in perspective. Look at the world rather than a screen whenever you can.

Disconnect after hours. Really let work go when you're off the clock, whether it's evening or the weekend. Use your non-work time to recharge fully by mentally unplugging from your job, and from your computer and phone. Try different activities to see what helps you the most—it's all about what makes you feel recharged.

Get moving to recover your energy. Physical activities like exercise are a great way to unwind. Moving your body can help you relax and recover from a long day. My favorite way to contemplate the day and unwind is to put on some earphones, turn on some heavy metal, and lift weights for an hour every day.

Take care of your mental recovery, even on tough days. Even if you're wiped out or stressed, try to start a recovery activity, as Sonnentag suggests. Your brain needs to refresh itself as much as your body needs to move. A bit of time with friends, a hobby, or something relaxing like a puzzle or reading a book can really help. Even if you're not feeling your best when you get started, you may well feel better afterward.

If you're managing a team, you have to help them sustain themselves as well. It's a Circle of Relationships, remember, not a line. Creating a culture that values real relaxation helps the whole team stay energized, motivated, and ready to give their best. Support your team members' mental health and well-being.

Respect off-time. Managers should be cool with letting team members fully unplug when they're off the clock. Avoid messaging or calling after hours unless it's urgent. It's important for everyone to have that real uninterrupted time to recharge.

Encourage breaks during the day. Make sure the team feels free to take short breaks at work. Whether it's to stretch, grab a snack, or just clear their heads, these mini-breaks help keep people energized and less stressed.

Ease back after vacations. After someone returns from vacation, give them some breathing room to get back into the groove. Jumping right back in at full speed can kill the relaxing effects of their time away.

Provide chill spaces and outdoor areas. Create spaces where people can take a break or recharge. In the same way you plan your clients' comfort, plan your team's: Consider cozy corners, break rooms, or outdoor spots where people can unwind. A little fresh air or a comfy space can make all the difference.

Encourage flexibility for personal downtime. Support people in managing their work schedules so that they can balance work with time for themselves, family, or hobbies. This helps everyone keep a healthy boundary between work and their personal life.

Lead by example with downtime. Managers should set the tone by also taking breaks, disconnecting after hours, and respecting their own boundaries. When the team sees leaders taking downtime seriously, it sends the message that it's okay for them to do the same.

Provide resources for wellness. If possible, offer resources like wellness programs, fitness reimbursements, or mental health support. When team members feel supported in their wellness goals, they're more likely to stay balanced and bring their best selves to work.

The Circle of Relationships runs deep. Your clients, team members, and suppliers need you to be emotionally mature and lead generously, and that starts and ends with taking care of yourself.

Building great relationships is a key step in finding your way to our last circle, the Circle of Fulfillment.

CIRCLE SIX

FULFILLMENT

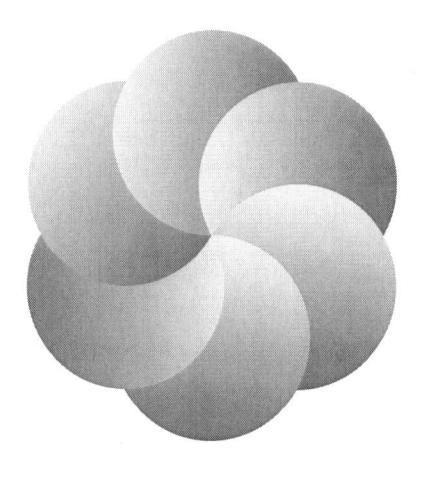

FULFILLMENT THRIVES in an infinite loop—when we give kindness, love, and purpose to others, it comes back to us in unexpected and meaningful ways. The more we contribute to the world, the more enriched we become, reinforcing a never-ending cycle of joy.

The Circle of Fulfillment is just that: a circle you build around what makes you and your clients feel fulfilled so that you're always focused on addressing the most important needs and, simultaneously, reaching your most heartfelt goal.

I want to be independent and fulfilled according to the Circle of Vision I've set out for myself. I want the same for my team members within my Circles of Trust and Focus, and for my clients in alignment with my Circles of Value and Relationships.

But the Circle of Fulfillment matters equally because fulfillment is a critical and infinite human need. What's the point of living life if you don't have the opportunity to feel fulfilled every day? If you can't bear setting the alarm clock to get up and go to work in the morning? If you don't have the time to share the best years of your life with your friends and family? You need to feel good if you want your Circle of Fulfillment to feel good.

Even if you aren't perfectly fulfilled right now, I want you to see fulfillment as your future. I want you to be able to imagine the life you want, and achieve that for yourself and for all of your circle.

Don't take it for granted that entrepreneurship has to be a slog.

21

Put People Before Everything

A FAMILY WITH a two-year-old son spent a weekend at Ritz-Carlton's Dove Mountain resort near Tucson, Arizona. As they were packing up to head to the airport, the child's mom realized that her son's favorite toy, Thomas the Tank Engine, was missing.

Total disaster for a toddler, right? The woman tracked down two Ritz employees, Jessy Long and Nathan Cliff, and told them how much this little toy meant to her son and how heartbroken he'd be without it.

Long and Cliff searched everywhere but couldn't find Thomas. Instead of giving up, though, they decided to do something special.

After the family left, they went to a toy store and found a perfect match for the missing Thomas. But they didn't stop there—they wrote a note in the voice of Thomas explaining to the little boy that he'd just gone on an extra adventure after getting left behind. They even took adorable photos of the new Thomas exploring the resort, cooking in the Ritz kitchen, and more.

Four days later, the toy arrived in the mail, and the family was blown away. They told everyone they knew and shared the story all over social media.

It's a story that's often repeated in business circles as well, and for good reason. The fact is that Long and Cliff created a Circle of Fulfillment out of a seemingly devastating situation for a small child. It was a success for the family, for Long and Cliff, and for the Ritz-Carlton as a brand. All of the stakeholders in this scenario went away happy.

Why? Because the employees put people before anything else.

Long and Cliff didn't just brush off the missing toy or say, "Sorry, nothing we can do." They took the time to understand how important it was to the toddler and how upset he would be by its loss.

Instead of giving up when they couldn't find the toy, they went out of their way to replace it. They even thought through the experience from the little boy's perspective, making it not just a replacement but a magical adventure that Thomas went on just for him. By taking that extra step, they showed that they truly cared—not just about routine service, but about making the family feel valued and understood.

MANY YEARS ago, when I took time out to attend Disney University in Orlando, Florida, I had the good fortune to meet Dennis Snow.

Snow worked in frontline operations, management, and customer service before moving to the Disney Institute, where he helped train people from other companies in the Disney way. His expertise comes from being on the ground and learning how Disney's approach isn't just about giving people what they expect—it's about giving them more than they ever thought possible. He understands the intentionality behind every detail, from how cast members (Disney's term for employees) interact with guests to the way each theme park is designed to create immersive, magical environments.

Snow is a joy to listen to. I've attended his classes and read his book. I've even invited him on my own podcast. Why? With so many years dedicated to working at Disney, Snow understands exactly how its parks continue to thrill and delight people over a hundred years after its founding as a company. He emphasizes that Disney's success lies in consistency and an unwavering focus on the customer experience.

To Disney, every single visitor matters, and Snow's insight is that keeping people delighted for over a century takes a mix of storytelling, anticipating customer needs, and focusing on every tiny detail.

Here's a story he shared with me.

Each year, several hundred people lose their car keys when visiting a Disney resort. Imagine it: You've spent a full day walking around one of Disney's massive amusement parks, the kids are exhausted and cranky, and all you want is to get back to your hotel. But when you reach into your pocket for your car keys—nothing.

Panic starts to set in. All those new and magical memories are suddenly overshadowed by the dread of being stranded.

But Disney's got you covered. Attendants are stationed throughout the parking lot, ready to help. If you let them know your keys are missing, they'll walk you to your car, grab your vehicle ID number, and head back to their station.

Here's the cool part: They're connected to a satellite system that links them to major car manufacturers around the world. Within twenty minutes, they can cut a new key for you or provide a digital signal to unlock and start your car.

That's a serious *wow* moment! Disney goes above and beyond to make sure even a potential nightmare like losing your keys ends on a high note.

THE MORAL of these two stories? If you can make toddlers happy under the most adverse conditions, you know exactly what it means to create a Circle of Fulfillment.

I'm joking. But I'm also not joking.

Putting people before everything means understanding that not everyone in your circle is going to be happy every day. And that's not just toddlers—many adults, when they're tired and frustrated, are also impatient and have a short attention span. Creating a Circle of Fulfillment means understanding that frustration on a gut level.

I'm sure you can easily empathize with someone in a situation where something has gone terribly wrong. They may have slipped and broken their arm, dropped a cup of coffee on their new couch, or seen their child fall off a slide in the park.

When things go wrong, you need the people around you to recognize your humanity, not your fear.

I am always happy to help other people. In my career, I've been able to give financial advice to every client, and career advice to every team member. I've made others very happy because they feel secure in their relationship with me. It's how my business has secured goodwill from clients, built a large network of some of the top financial advisors in the world, and retained the best employees in the industry.

Putting people first isn't just about big gestures or quick fixes; it's also about recognizing that sometimes people around you are going through tough moments. Being there for them at those times shows that you truly care.

Here are four ways to build your Circle of Fulfillment by putting people first. These ideas apply not just to your clients, but to everyone in your life.

Listen without judgment. When someone's having a rough day, sometimes they just need to vent. Instead of offering solutions or saying "it'll be okay," try just listening. Let them express their feelings without any interruptions. When people tell me I could do something better, I don't make excuses. This makes them feel heard and respected.

Ask, don't assume. Instead of guessing what they need, I ask people directly what it is. I proactively ask them if they are having problems that I can solve. A simple "How can I support you right now?" can go a long way. It shows you're genuinely interested in helping in a way that works for them, not just what you think would help.

Give them space if they need it. Sometimes, people need a little room to process what they're feeling. I give them the time they need to reflect and make decisions on their own rather than pressuring them for an answer, even if my business would run more smoothly knowing that answer sooner. Respecting their boundaries and letting them know you're there for them whenever they're ready can be incredibly comforting.

Offer small gestures of kindness. Simple actions like bringing them their favorite coffee or sending a quick message to check in can make a big difference. I make the time to ask and remember what matters to others. Small acts of personal acknowledgment show that you're thinking of them and care about their well-being.

22

Scale Like Schultz

HAVE YOU ever visited Seattle? Besides its great music scene, the city is home to some pretty legendary businesses. One spot that draws huge crowds is Pike Place Market, right by the waterfront. As you wander through the market, you might notice a line stretching down the block. Follow that line and soon you'll find yourself at the very first Starbucks. (Technically it's the second location, but it's the oldest one still standing.)

Now, if you're not into business, this might just seem like a cool tourist stop. But for anyone studying how to scale a company, this place is pure inspiration. Howard Schultz, the man who made Starbucks what it is today, started with that single coffee shop. The Pike Place location became his prototype, the testing ground where he developed and refined the concept of Starbucks as we know it.

Schultz's vision was to bring the Italian coffee shop experience to America. That meant not just serving coffee, but perfecting everything—the look, the service, even the smell of the store. He and his team spent a lot of time getting this right. Of course they focused on the types of coffee they would serve, but they didn't stop there. They experimented with the layout, the uniforms, the logo, and the atmosphere. They paid close attention to what customers liked, asking for feedback constantly and making tweaks based on what they'd learned.

The goal was to create a place that people would want to come back to—a cozy, inviting "third place" between home and work. Starbucks wanted to be the spot where people could relax, meet friends, or get some work done. They perfected this model at Pike Place before they even thought about expanding.

Once they felt they had the right formula, they started to scale. First they opened more stores in Seattle, and then moved into other cities. With each new location, they continued to refine their process, learning from what worked and what didn't. They closed stores that weren't profitable and opened new ones in locations where they saw potential.

As of 2024, Starbucks had over 39,000 stores worldwide and a market capitalization of around $107 billion. Schultz took the time to perfect his concept on a small scale and then expanded it on a massive one, while staying true to the experience that made Starbucks special in the first place.

PROBABLY THE number one question I get is this: How can I scale my business?

The reason it's so common is that scaling is the hardest part of building a business. Every company reaches its ceiling of complexity at some point. This is when it ceases to grow because there isn't much more that can be done to renew its capacity without tearing it apart. Businesses at this stage attract new clients infrequently, and net profits may continue to grow at single-digit levels or not at all.

When that happens, you have to make some very bold decisions.

In my own business, I have reached the ceiling of complexity more than once. And when it happened, I made changes to overcome our inertia.

Those changes were always about people, because both my brand and my services are about people. At a constriction point, I would look at what needed to get done to make my clients happy, and then I'd find the best people to run and grow each area of the business.

There are, of course, other ways to scale, like using technological advances to make your processes easier, simplifying your product line, aligning your sales and engagement opportunities, and rationalizing reporting lines. But ultimately, scaling up your business is about you.

Two of my favorite books are Michael Gerber's *The E-Myth* and its follow-up, *The E-Myth Revisited*. These books offer a powerful lesson on the difference between a practitioner and an entrepreneur in building a business. (Hint: Howard Schultz is an entrepreneur.)

Gerber explains that practitioners and entrepreneurs have entirely different approaches. Practitioners build a business around themselves and their skills. They're often the hands-on expert who knows their craft inside and out, so they end up doing everything themselves. The result? The business depends heavily on them to operate, and it's challenging to step back without everything falling apart. Think back to my example of Pete's Donuts. Practitioners can feel trapped because they're central to every task, and growth becomes limited by their personal capacity.

Entrepreneurs, on the other hand, build a business around processes, Gerber writes. Instead of doing everything personally, they focus on creating systems that deliver a consistent, high-quality experience for customers no matter who's running the day-to-day operations. This approach makes it possible to replicate the business over and over—think franchises or chain stores. Entrepreneurs are focused on scalability, which allows them to step back as the business grows.

The takeaway from *The E-Myth* is clear: If you want to grow a business that doesn't rely solely on you, think like an entrepreneur. Focus on processes that ensure quality and can be duplicated, creating consistent success even without your constant involvement.

So, how does this apply to your Circle of Fulfillment? Using an entrepreneurial growth plan makes fulfillment possible for everyone.

Before you try to grow big, make sure you've perfected your concept and then create a system around it. Test it out, refine it, and listen to your customers. Make adjustments until you're confident in your formula. Once you have something that works, then start scaling. Duplicate the formula in new locations or add new products, but always keep an eye on what's working and be willing to make changes.

Scaling up isn't just about getting bigger; it's about building smart, sustainable growth based on a proven formula. That's how you go from one small shop to a global brand. Here are three specific ideas for doing this.

Start by making a list of all of your business's crucial tasks. Include everything from customer interactions to back-end processes, and for each task ask yourself: What's the outcome I want to achieve? This helps clarify the purpose and set standards for each one, guiding how you design and perform it.

Break down each task into a series of steps that can be followed in the same order every time. Essentially, you're creating a user manual for each task. When building each system, keep two key things in mind: simplicity and consistency. Focus on the minimum number of steps needed to achieve the best result, making the system clear and straightforward enough for anyone to follow effectively.

Train and delegate. Once these systems are in place, you can train staff to use them exactly as they're documented. This means that even if you delegate tasks, your team can follow the same steps with confidence and accuracy, maintaining the high standards you've set. With this consistency, you can feel confident that customers are experiencing the best version of your business every time. And as a leader, you gain back valuable time that you can put toward strategic growth and other high-level priorities.

Take the example in chapter 16 of a sales presentation designed to gain new clients. The goal is to help clients understand the value you bring to their families. To systematize this, think about the questions potential clients might have and answer them ahead of time. Design a sales presentation that's easy to customize to each client but still follows a repeatable, structured format. This system should allow you to quickly personalize the presentation for any new prospect while ensuring that every client gets a polished, well-thought-out experience. Instead of "winging it" or varying your approach each time, you can pull up your standardized presentation, make a few adjustments, and be ready to deliver a consistent, high-quality experience.

Creating a complete system for each task saves time and ensures a professional approach in every customer interaction. Plus, it's a huge asset as your business grows.

The beauty of well-designed systems is that they bring consistency and reliability to every area of your business. Which is the key to your Circle of Fulfillment.

23

Put Passion Before Work

AFTER WORKING at the farm with my father for a few summers in my high school years, I packed my car and drove down to Miami.

I had saved up all of my farm earnings to get there. As I mentioned in chapter 1, it was where I wanted to be. *Miami Vice*'s Crockett and Tubbs had made it look like the coolest place on Earth. They patrolled the streets like rock stars rather than police detectives, and they seemed to know everyone and everything.

When I arrived, my dream came true almost immediately. I was cast as an extra in a *Miami Vice* episode. I'd seen an ad calling for people for crowd scenes, and the pay was a hundred bucks. But more importantly for a young guy without much money, they gave you all the food you could eat. I made it my job to suss out places that had cheap food, like bars, buffets, and movie sets. At the craft services buffet, I loaded my pockets up before I left for the day.

My main job, just like at home, was working on the track. Because my father trained racehorses, I had an in. I found out I could get US working papers as a part of a sports team, and horse racing counted. For nine months, I slogged at the racetrack during the day and played poker in the evenings. Because I had played cards my whole teenage life, I made as much money at the poker table as I did working with horses. But I also knew exactly where the ten-cent wings were, and that I could get a plate full of free tacos if I bought a single beer.

I lived in Miami for about nine months, until I moved back many years later. But the city was a little rougher in those days than my hometown, Toronto. I was passionate about Miami, and then, suddenly, I wasn't. I started to feel unsafe. The cocaine cowboy wars were raging, and it was getting shady at the track, so I upped stakes and went home, jaded and a bit tougher.

I LEARNED some lessons in Miami, but I learned them the easy way. Some people learn lessons by going through almost unimaginable hardship.

Viktor Frankl lived through four different Nazi concentration camps.

A Holocaust survivor and later a therapist, Frankl turned his greatest challenge into his greatest asset. He had already been working in the field of psychiatry, treating the chronically depressed, when he was captured by the Nazis along with his family, all of whom—except for him—were killed. In the camps, Frankl was both prisoner and caretaker. Separated from his parents and his wife, he tended to others as he kept himself focused on what he could do to remain sane and well. As much as he could, he worked.

In his work, providing medical and therapeutic care to others, Frankl found hope. Even in the harshest and most hopeless situations, he began to understand, people can survive and find purpose.

Frankl believed that our drive to find meaning is the deepest human motivation, and he saw this search for purpose as a guiding force that can keep us going no matter the obstacles.

Why is Frankl's story important? Because his ideas aren't just about surviving extreme hardship—they're incredibly relevant to your future as an entrepreneur.

Some of our personal and professional hardships are extreme, and others less so. And no matter what specialization you choose, if you're an entrepreneur you're already taking a difficult path forward. But if you create a career for yourself based on what you're passionate about, you're already tapping into a source of meaning. Frankl teaches us that if your work is rooted in something you truly care about, it will help you push through tough times because you're driven by more than just money or status—you're doing it because it feels worthwhile and meaningful.

Starting a business is rarely easy. You'll face setbacks, stress, and uncertainty. But if your "why" is strong and rooted in what you love, that purpose will keep you motivated. Frankl's message is clear: Meaning can help us adapt and keep going. So, when passion fuels your business, you're not only likely to stick with it but also more likely to create something truly impactful—something that aligns with who you are and the change you want to make in the world.

For this reason, most of your life should be spent on your passions, not your work. To remain in the Circle of Fulfillment, you have to come back to your passions, or else every day at work will feel like hell and you'll face diminishing returns.

It's true that what you do for work and what you're passionate about can be two different things. What matters is that the hours you spend working have meaning.

———————

YOU CAN and should be different and unique, the real version of yourself, if you want to be successful in business. This is where the Circle of Fulfillment links up with every other circle in this book. Being successful in business isn't about fitting into a box; it's about redefining the box, or even throwing it away entirely.

Trying to be like everyone else just isn't going to get you anywhere special. In the business world, the best thing you can bring to the table is *you*—the real, unfiltered version of yourself. Why? Because that's the one thing no one else has. If you're out there, putting your unique spin on things and speaking honestly about what you believe in, that's when people start to take notice.

Instead of seeing your job as the end-all, think of it as the thing that helps you chase what you love outside of work. Let me sum up my own passion in three easy points.

1. My goal wasn't to be a wealth management entrepreneur; it was to be able to afford spending my winters in a warm place.

2. I found that I loved wealth management as a side effect of my passion, but it had the same impact on my life.

3. I built meaning out of the part of wealth management that mattered most to me, which was spending time with people.

That's it. It was that simple to create my Circle of Fulfillment.

Research says this shift in perspective can make a big difference for the people you manage as well. When people see their job as a way to fund their passion projects, they're more likely to stay productive and mentally healthy in the long run.

Why? Because having that outlet—whether it's a side gig, a hobby, or a life goal—keeps people feeling empowered and positive. It's like a boost that spills over into their day job. They're bringing good vibes and engagement from their passion back into the workplace, which keeps them happy and performing well. Jobs that give employees some breathing room for other pursuits not only attract talent but retain staff because they're energized and engaged.

So, maybe the way forward isn't just about work-life *balance*; it's about creating the space for work to be a launchpad for the stuff that truly lights you up.

IT'S HEALTHY for you, and for everyone else, to keep your personal goals in mind every day on the job.

So, let's identify where you derive your sense of meaning in life. As you learned long ago in elementary school, you can define a circle with three points. Here are the three points that will define your Circle of Fulfillment—what are they for you?

What's your actual goal? I don't mean the job you want to have—what is the *life* you want to have? Imagine what it would feel like to live in a number of different places, or a variety of ways. What feels the best to you? What feels onerous or tiresome? Eliminate what doesn't work and focus in on what does. Write down your actual life goal in as much detail as possible.

How can you achieve your chosen life goal? Write down all of the possible pathways forward. Be critical—eliminate the paths that have no chance of working out. If you're in business already, what kind of clients do you need? Do you want to spend time increasing your education or skills? What products and services could allow you to get there?

What matters most to you on a day-to-day basis? Consider how you can create meaning in the work you have to do to achieve your goal. What is the one thing that will continue to get you excited about your work, even on the worst day? Explore how you can build your work around that sense of meaning in what you do.

Once you've defined your points, it's time to draw your Circle of Fulfillment.

24

Roll Forward or Roll Back

IN A book called *The Making of a Blockbuster*, author Gail DeGeorge details the work and life of an entrepreneur named Wayne Huizenga.

In one aspect of his career, Huizenga was a lot like me. He was focused on how to solve his customers' problems more than anything else. How did he do it? By looking at what a company did best and adding volume.

Huizenga started with garbage collection, buying up local waste management companies and turning them into Waste Management Inc., one of the largest companies of its kind in the world. Later, he did something similar with AutoNation, consolidating used car dealerships under one brand and setting up a huge connected car sales infrastructure across the US. He also bought up local video stores and rebranded them under the name Blockbuster, building on each store's strengths and creating an industry giant.

In each business he developed, Huizenga created a service delivery system. This solved customers' problems by making services more reliable and best practices more replicable. He fulfilled orders. He fulfilled customer values. No matter what service branch customers walked into, they'd be offered a level of fulfillment they hadn't experienced before.

I built my company, Investment Planning Counsel, by employing the same strategy Huizenga had used: buying up smaller mutual fund dealerships and merging them together.

The strategy of "rolling up" a series of businesses is pretty straightforward in theory—you buy a bunch of similar firms, combine their strengths, cut the extras, and build a bigger, more efficient company.

Say you're buying smaller businesses at three times their revenue, which is a common rule of thumb. By merging them under a single brand with a unified strategy, that combined business could end up being worth *ten* times the revenue. That's the magic of a successful roll-up: You take something small, make it part of something much bigger and more efficient, and create value that goes far beyond what you paid for each piece.

It sounds straightforward, but actually doing it can be surprisingly tough. Why?

Because you can't get big at the expense of customer value.

GETTING BACK to basics is the key to growing your business. Not surprisingly, you have to come full circle to complete your Circle of Fulfillment. This means clearing out barriers to growth and imagining a different future.

For example, when you're thinking about buying out a competitor to grow your long-term profitability, there's one critical rule you can't ignore: Your own business needs to be running better than the one you're buying. Otherwise you're just stacking one shaky business on top of another, and it's not going to magically turn into a success.

I see people break this rule all the time because they think they can jump into the Circle of Fulfillment with money, rather than strategy.

Folks see buying another business as an easy way to get more clients and quickly expand. But as I tell people coming up in the wealth management field, if your business isn't streamlined and profitable yet, buying a struggling competitor isn't going to fix that. If you lack consistency of service and have no standard processes, no communication plan, and no real strategy for future profitability, then you'd do better to go back to the beginning of this book and start a quest for authenticity, value creation, and relationship building. In fact, you may need a new Circle of Vision to map out a new road to success if you're going to start rolling up.

Another barrier to growth is that people make a lot of false assumptions because they're focused on what *they* think is important, which their customers may not think is important at all.

That's when their business stops growing and it makes no sense to buy another.

For example, when wealth management advisors target individuals with high net worth, they often assume that these customers are looking for better investment solutions. Sure, they need decent, reliable offerings. But what they're really looking for is advice about taxation, estate planning, how to look after their family, and how to live a great life, free of worry. They also want to have a single point of contact, someone they communicate with on a regular basis.

The best way to figure out exactly which problems you want to solve for the next iteration of your business is to ask your customers. In particular, talk to customers who are looking to build their own businesses and scale them to the next level. Devise a step-by-step implementation plan to help them get where they want to go so that you can spend some time imagining how you're going to build your own future plans.

Where are the gaps in your business offerings, and what might help you get better before you get bigger?

Another key point is that the more another business looks like yours, the more valuable it is to you. Why is that? Because you want to bring ease and simplicity to growth, not force really disparate business plans together. And remember, to acquire a business you need a well-oiled machine first—clear processes, consistent and valuable customer offerings, a solid communication plan, and a path for growth. Only then will you be ready to take on another business and turn it into something better.

ONLY ONCE you've cleared your path can you follow the three essential steps to rolling up a new business into your own.

You're probably not ready to grow big right this minute, but having an overview of what to expect means you can set your own stage for success. The goal is twofold: to ensure everyone gets enough of what they want, and to set the foundation for a smooth transition. Your strategy should be focused on delivering a unified client experience at the end of the process.

The deal. Start by defining what you're looking for in a potential acquisition, then list businesses that fit those criteria. Many people think deals will just land in their laps, but the truth is you need to put in the work up front to get conversations going with potential sellers. Network through your existing Circle of Relationships and let people know you're a capable, reliable buyer who will take good care of their business and clients. When it comes to closing the deal, it's about reaching terms that work for both sides. This means agreeing on a fair price based on revenue and reducing risks like client loss, compliance issues, and staffing challenges.

Integration. Once you've closed the deal, the next stage is integrating the acquired business into your own. A full overhaul may not be necessary on day one, but there should be a clear, gradual plan to bring everything in line between the two companies. Remember, if you're in a service business like wealth management, the value your acquisition brings to the table is in their people and relationships with their customers. Change will be hard for the selling company's team, so when you're bringing new people into your own way of operating, you'll want to tread carefully. Integration means aligning systems, human resources policies, incentive structures, communication strategies, and, importantly, the client experience. For a wealth management business, for instance, you should also plan to consolidate client holdings in a way that reflects your own investment philosophy.

Facilitation. The third stage is all about facilitating the transition so that it runs smoothly and setting up the structure for future growth. Once you've aligned systems and processes, focus on maintaining a seamless operation and helping the newly acquired team adapt to the unified way of doing things. This includes ongoing training, setting expectations, and fostering a collaborative culture.

Being transparent in your approach helps you and your potential acquisitions align on the values that serve customers' needs. It also creates an impetus for a less-than-perfect business to up their game so that they'll be more valuable to you over the long term.

Without a strong plan, you'll end up with a mismatched collection of businesses that drain profitability and hinder growth, which is the exact opposite of what you aimed to achieve with a roll-up. By carefully managing each stage—finding the right deals, ensuring seamless integration, and setting up a sustainable framework—you'll have a much stronger chance of creating a scalable, profitable business that grows efficiently.

And that, my friends, builds value, consistency, and long-term strength, giving your Circle of Fulfillment a powerful foundation.

25

Remember the Circle of Life

I HAVE A tattoo with the Latin inscription *memento mori*. It's a call for me to remember that in the circle of life, everyone, including me, must eventually die.

It's not as morbid as it sounds. It's a call to action, and it's an idea that has stayed with me throughout my life. As spiritual teacher Ram Dass writes, the fact that death exists is a reminder to live fully in the moment. It's a reminder to lose yourself in the love of your own journey.

That reminder rings true when I think about my personal hero, the chef Anthony Bourdain. For years, I watched all his shows, read all his books, and followed his life. When he took his own life, I was as devastated as I would have been if he were a family member. From where I sat, here was a guy who lived an exciting life. He got to travel to exotic locations, meet interesting people from different cultures, eat delicious food, and drink great wine.

That's what I want to do, I thought in 2018 as I read his obituary.

But my next thought was this: *When?*

I was running a company. There were a lot of responsibilities on my plate. The role of a president and CEO meant constant meetings—board meetings, operational meetings, regulatory meetings, and other demands on my time every moment of the day. And, if I can let you in on a little secret, I hate meetings. I know that if I were really true to myself and wanted to pursue my dream of real freedom, I would have to make a change.

Luckily, I had set myself up for freedom. But let me take a step back for a moment.

In my work, I talk to many entrepreneurs who never find freedom. They never pursue the really important things in life, instead completely identifying their persona as their business role. As I write this book, I just received news about a well-known colleague in the wealth management business who was sitting at his desk on a Tuesday and had a massive heart attack. He died at the relatively young age of sixty. He is not the first or last person to do so in the working world. After a long and prosperous career, some entrepreneurs, just as they are about to enjoy the fruits of their labor, experience something completely unexpected that derails all those well-intentioned plans.

There is a life alongside business. You have the ability to define and then redefine what you do at every moment of every day. You can widen your circles to include more people, more opportunities, and more fulfillment. You can focus on the things that you truly enjoy doing: things that inspire you, make you happy, and engage you for hours. Your life is something malleable.

If you start with your true vision, clearly defined, and then build out each circle, you will create trust, keep your work focused, create true value for everyone around you, and build deep and meaningful relationships. Then you will have come back to what it's all about: fulfillment.

Your life will come first, just as mine has.

After years of acquiring, integrating, and leading companies, I have come full circle in my career, having taken on the role of executive chair at Investment Planning Counsel with a renewed sense of purpose and fulfillment. This transition was not just a shift in structure, but a strategic alignment between my Circles of Vision, Trust, Focus, Value, and Relationships, which define my professional and personal philosophy. All of these elements come together in my Circle of Fulfillment, the ultimate integration of purpose, impact, and success. This holistic approach ensures that my work remains meaningful, my partnerships remain strong, and my business ecosystem continues to thrive.

For years I planned my career around reaching my ultimate goal—freedom. Freedom means many different things to people, but for me, I wanted freedom to travel and live in other countries. Knowing this was what I wanted, I developed skills on the selling side of my business and not the buying side. As executive chair of IPC, I created a role of my own design. I spend time with advisors helping them build a better business and mentoring their work. I focused on creating exceptional client experiences.

As I sit on my balcony in Miami, I am surrounded by symbols of my six circles, each reflecting a core principle of my journey. The sun shines warmly on me—a reminder of fulfillment, the energy that fuels my purpose. On my finger, my wedding ring represents relationships, the deep connections that sustain and inspire me. In my pocket, coins serve as a tangible reflection of value, the wealth of both financial success and meaningful contributions. My phone, resting face down with its camera lens visible, embodies focus, the discipline to direct attention to where it matters most. As I gaze over the ocean, its stillness and depth mirror trust, communication, and the foundation of lasting partnerships and leadership.

And above all, I see this entire scene through my own eye—a symbol of vision, the clarity and perspective that guide every decision I make. These six circles are not just concepts; they are ever present, shaping how I experience and navigate the world around me.

Every day of my life has been worth living, and it's only getting better.

I live fully in the moment, and I have given myself the gift of an extraordinary life of freedom.

What's your gift to yourself going to be? Remember what's at stake, and remember that your vision will take you where you want to go.

Live free now.

Acknowledgments

I WANT TO START BY thanking my wife and partner-in-crime, Tessa, for constantly reminding me that life is about the experiences we build together. As important as work may be, the true goal is freedom.

I also want to thank my group of dysfunctional friends and family, who are a constant source of love and entertainment. I give deep thanks to my Mommy, for giving birth to yours truly and instilling the love of reading and education.

Thank you to the great team at Page Two for the development and production of this book. It could not have been done without everyone's help. I thank the amazing Lisa Thomas-Tench for doing all the really hard work, and my editor, James Harbeck, for bringing it all together.

Of course, this book would not have been possible without the help and support of my Team Awesome. I must thank the entire team at Investment Planning Counsel, starting with the leadership team that I have had the privilege to work with over our many years in business. Together I think we built something pretty special.

A special shout-out to my long-suffering but incredible assistant, Gayle Sullivan. I couldn't have done it without you.

And finally, I want to thank the hard-working financial advisors who have been associated with Investment Planning Counsel over the years. It is an honorable profession that continues to make the lives of clients better and allow them to live their dreams. I have learned so much from all of you, and every day you should be proud of what you do. You have inspired me more than you can ever imagine.

Notes

Chapter 2: Fall in Love

16   *adults fear they'll never get passionate*: Paul A. O'Keefe, Carol S. Dweck, and Gregory M. Walton, "Implicit Theories of Interest: Finding Your Passion or Developing It?" *Psychological Science* 29, no. 10 (2018): 1653–1664.

16   *They conducted another study*: Paul A. O'Keefe et al., "A Growth-Theory-of-Interest Intervention Increases Interest in Math and Science Coursework Among Liberal Arts Undergraduates," *Journal of Educational Psychology* 115, no. 6 (2023): 859.

Chapter 3: Get on Your Quest

22   *test their own limits and to eventually succeed*: Michael D. Mrazek et al., "Pushing the Limits: Cognitive, Affective, and Neural Plasticity Revealed by an Intensive Multifaceted Intervention," *Frontiers in Human Neuroscience* 10 (2016): 180423.

22   *Successful CEOs may be depressed*: Ron A. Carucci, "Why Success Doesn't Lead to Satisfaction," *Harvard Business Review*, January 25, 2023, https://hbr.org/2023/01/why-success-doesnt-lead-to-satisfaction; Michael A. Freeman et al., "The Prevalence and Co-occurrence of Psychiatric Conditions Among Entrepreneurs and Their Families," *Small Business Economics* 53, no. 2 (2019): 323–342.

23 *more neural connections mean greater brain power*: Allison Lundy and Jeffrey Trawick-Smith, "Effects of Active Outdoor Play on Preschool Children's On-Task Classroom Behavior," *Early Childhood Education Journal* 49, no. 3 (2021): 463–471; Ulrich Dettweiler et al., "Choice Matters: Pupils' Stress Regulation, Brain Development and Brain Function in an Outdoor Education Project," *British Journal of Educational Psychology* 93, no. S1 (2023): 152–173.

23 *the hero's journey*: Joseph Campbell, *The Hero with a Thousand Faces* (Pantheon Books, 1949).

26 *"Victorious warriors win first and then go to war"*: Sun Tzu, *The Art of War*, chapter 4: "Tactical Dispositions."

Chapter 4: Be Like Arnold

29 *"I want to be a staarrr!"*: *Arnold*, directed by Lesley Chilcott, Defiant Ones Media Group, Invented by Girls, and Netflix, 2023.

31 *keep clear of unreachable ones*: Gabriele Oettingen and Klaus Michael Reininger, "The Power of Prospection: Mental Contrasting and Behavior Change," *Social and Personality Psychology Compass* 10, no. 11 (2016): 591–604.

Circle Two: Trust

38 *a 20 percent increase in customer loyalty*: NielsenIQ, "Label Insight 2021," industry report, https://nielseniq.com/global/en/landing-page/label-insight.

38 *50 percent more productivity*: Paul J. Zak, "The Neuroscience of Trust," *Harvard Business Review*, January–February 2017, https://hbr.org/2017/01/the-neuroscience-of-trust.

38 *"It helped me build credibility"*: Zak, "The Neuroscience of Trust."

Chapter 5: Find Your Plumbers

41 *"knowing its boundaries, however, is vital"*: David Cancel, "Charlie Munger and Warren Buffett Use This Mental Model to Stay Focused on Their Strengths," *Inc.*, May 30, 2019, https://www.inc.com/david-cancel/charlie-munger-warren-buffett-use-this-mental-model-to-stay-focused-on-their-strengths.html.

41 *In 2005, Switzerland-based researchers*: W. Chan Kim and Renée Mauborgne, *Blue Ocean Strategy* (Harvard Business Review Press, 2005).

42   *work is best understood as a lifelong journey:* Wolfgang Mayrhofer and Hugh Gunz, "From Wallflower to Life and Soul of the Party: Acknowledging Time's Role at Center Stage in the Study of Careers," *International Journal of Human Resource Management* 34, no. 3 (2023): 562–604.

Chapter 6: Solve Obvious Problems

45   *businesses would fail*: David Martin, "FedEx: A 50-year revolution of business," CBS News, June 4, 2023, https://www.cbsnews.com/news/federal-express-fred-smith-50-years-of-fedex.

45   *Steve Jobs was out for a jog*: John Waters, "Want More Sales? Simple. Create a Problem, Then Solve It," Waters Business Consulting Group, October 10, 2022, https://watersbusinessconsulting.com/2021/10/22/want-more-sales-simple-create-a-problem-then-solve-it.

45   *limited in its ability to present their wares*: Jean-Louis Barsoux, Michael Wade, and Cyril Bouquet, "Identifying Unmet Needs in a Digital Age," *Harvard Business Review*, July–August 2022, https://hbr.org/2022/07/identifying-unmet-needs-in-a-digital-age.

47   *questions that are catalytic*: Eric Brown, "Asking the Questions That Unlock Innovation," *MIT News*, April 6, 2018, https://news.mit.edu/2018/mit-leadership-center-hal-gregersen-asking-questions-that-unlock-innovation-0406.

Chapter 7: Decide If You're Pete's Donuts or Tim Hortons

51   *one hundred times as much coffee as Starbucks*: Statista, Tim Hortons Revenue in USD (2024), https://www.statista.com/statistics/291507/annual-revenue-tim-hortons/; ZoomInfo, Starbucks Canada (2024), https://www.zoominfo.com/c/starbucks---the-independent/362039577.

53   *One of the most inspirational books*: Jim Collins, *Good to Great: Why Some Companies Make the Leap… And Others Don't* (HarperBusiness, 2011).

Chapter 8: Open the Window

61   *Gen Z and millennial customers*: Ashley Reichheld, John Peto, and Cory Ritthaler, "Research: Consumers' Sustainability Demands Are Rising," *Harvard Business Review*, September 18, 2023, https://hbr.org/2023/09/research-consumers-sustainability-demands-are-rising.

192   THE SIX CIRCLE STRATEGY

62   *Its sales have quadrupled*: Gabby Land, "Op-Ed: Patagonia Proves the Success of Sustainable Corporations," *Michigan Journal of Economics*, November 22, 2023, https://sites.lsa.umich.edu/mje/2023/11/22/op-ed-patagonia-proves-the-success-of-sustainable-corporations.

62   *trust in institutions is less than 50 percent*: Christine Lagarde, "There's a Reason for the Lack of Trust in Government and Business: Corruption," *IMF Blog*, May 4, 2018, https://www.imf.org/en/blogs/articles/2018/05/04/theres-a-reason-for-the-lack-of-trust-in-government-and-business-corruption.

Circle Three: Focus

68   *"Innovation is saying no to 1,000 things"*: Brandon Griggs, "10 Great Quotes from Steve Jobs," CNN, January 4, 2016, https://edition.cnn.com/2012/10/04/tech/innovation/steve-jobs-quotes/index.html.

Chapter 9: Don't Mess with Success

71   *Jeff Bezos once said*: Mark Ritson, "Jeff Bezos's Success at Amazon Is Down to One Thing: Focusing on the Customer,"*MarketingWeek*, February 3, 2021, https://www.marketingweek.com/mark-ritson-jeff-bezos-success-focusing-on-customer.

71   *the organization as a whole*: Joyce Falkenberg et al., "When Change Becomes Excessive," *Research in Organizational Change and Development* 15 (2005): 31–62.

Chapter 10: Outsource Catching Rabbits

77   *"maintaining an owner-oriented attitude"*: Olga Milicevic, "Laissez-faire leadership: Traits, benefits, & disadvantages," *Pumble*, August 29, 2023, https://pumble.com/blog/laissez-faire-leadership.

77   *"They know what needs to be done"*: "Learning from Southwest's Herb Kelleher," Investment Masters Class blog, January 12, 2019, https://mastersinvest.com/newblog/2019/1/9/learning-from-herb-kelleher.

Chapter 11: Read the Book

81   *developed over time with effort and learning*: Carol S. Dweck, *Mindset: The New Psychology of Success* (Random House, 2006).

81   *people often have three mistaken ideas*: Carol S. Dweck, "What Having a 'Growth Mindset' Actually Means," *Harvard Business Review*, January 13, 2016, https://hbr.org/2016/01/what-having-a-growth-mindset-actually-means.

83 *Feeling connected to a bigger purpose*: Paul J. Zak, "The Neuroscience of Trust," *Harvard Business Review*, January–February 2017, https://hbr.org/2017/01/the-neuroscience-of-trust.

86 *a perennial bestseller*: Stephen R. Covey, *The 7 Habits of Highly Effective People* (Simon & Schuster, 2020).

Chapter 13: Map the Little Things

102 *companies that are really good at personalization*: Deloitte, "Personalization: It's a Value Exchange Between Brands and Customers," 2024, https://www.deloittedigital.com/content/dam/digital/us/documents/insights/insights-20240610-personalization-report.pdf.

102 *McKinsey agrees*: Fernando Beltran et al., "The Secret to Delighting Customers," McKinsey & Company, December 1, 2015, https://www.mckinsey.com/capabilities/growth-marketing-and-sales/our-insights/the-secret-to-delighting-customers.

104 *Ritz-Carlton gives staff members*: Micah Solomon, "A Ritz-Carlton Caliber Customer Experience Requires Employee Empowerment and Customer Service Standards," *Forbes*, September 18, 2013, https://www.forbes.com/sites/micahsolomon/2013/09/18/empowered-employees-vs-brand-standards-the-customer-experience-needs-both.

Chapter 14: Communicate Constantly

106 *skills that foster a healthy marriage*: Diane Coutu, "Making Relationships Work," *Harvard Business Review*, December 2007, https://hbr.org/2007/12/making-relationships-work.

107 *"You prep like nothing else"*: Bill McNabb, Ram Charan, and Dennis Carey, "Engaging with Your Investors," *Harvard Business Review*, July–August 2021, https://hbr.org/2021/07/engaging-with-your-investors.

Chapter 15: Provide the Greatest Client Experience

114 *Lego sent researchers to actually live with families*: Christian Madsbjerg and Mikkel B. Rasmussen, "An Anthropologist Walks into a Bar…," *Harvard Business Review*, March 2014, https://hbr.org/2014/03/an-anthropologist-walks-into-a-bar.

114 *"people who like Legos for what Legos are"*: Madsbjerg and Rasmussen, "An Anthropologist Walks into a Bar…."

Chapter 17: Create Deep Relationships

131 *as if we're facing a threat*: James J. Gross and Robert W. Levenson, "Emotional Suppression: Physiology, Self-Report, and Expressive Behavior," *Journal of Personality and Social Psychology* 64, no. 6 (1993): 970.

Chapter 18: Don't Manage People

137 *"Orders and directions don't work"*: Rob Markey, *The Customer Confidential Podcast*, "Do You Want to Lead or Just Manage?" October 10, 2019, https://www.netpromotersystem.com/insights/do-you-want-to-lead-or-just-manage-nps-podcast.

138 *They don't use fear or pressure*: Jack Zenger and Joseph Folkman, "7 Things Leaders Do to Help People Change," *Harvard Business Review*, July 20, 2015, https://hbr.org/2015/07/7-things-leaders-do-to-help-people-change.

138 *it lights a fire*: Paul Kirkbride, "Developing Transformational Leaders: The Full Range Leadership Model in Action," *Industrial and Commercial Training* 38, no. 1 (2006): 23–32.

141 *"in the people business serving coffee"*: Howard Behar and Janet Goldstein, *It's Not About the Coffee: Lessons on Putting People First from a Life at Starbucks* (Portfolio, 2007).

Chapter 19: Keep Raving Fans, Drop the Rest

145 *the power of raving fans*: Nassim Nicholas Taleb, *Antifragile: How to Live in a World We Don't Understand* (Allen Lane, 2012).

Chapter 20: Sustain Yourself

150 *Stepping away from work is crucial*: Sabine Sonnentag, Bonnie Hayden Cheng, and Stacey L. Parker, "Recovery from Work: Advancing the Field Toward the Future," *Annual Review of Organizational Psychology and Organizational Behavior* 9, no. 1 (2022): 33–60.

151 *"I could be outside enjoying this nice weather"*: Laura M. Giurge and Kaitlin Woolley, "Working During Non-Standard Work Time Undermines Intrinsic Motivation," *Organizational Behavior and Human Decision Processes* 170 (2022): 104134.

Chapter 21: Put People Before Everything

159 *Thomas the Tank Engine*: Micah Solomon, "Heroic Customer Service: When Ritz-Carlton Saved Thomas the Tank Engine," *Forbes*, January 15, 2015, https://www.forbes.com/sites/micahsolomon/2015/01/15/the-amazing-true-story-of-the-hotel-that-saved-thomas-the-tank-engine.

161 *I've attended his classes and read his book*: Dennis Snow, *Lessons from the Mouse: A Guide for Applying Disney World's Secrets of Success to Your Organization, Your Career, and Your Life* (Snow & Associates, 2010).

Chapter 22: Scale Like Schultz

167 *These books offer a powerful lesson*: Michael E. Gerber, *The E-Myth Revisited: Why Most Small Businesses Don't Work and What to Do About It* (HarperCollins, 2021).

Chapter 23: Put Passion Before Work

172 *he was captured by the Nazis*: Viktor E. Frankl, *Man's Search for Meaning* (Simon & Schuster, 1985).

175 *this shift in perspective*: Lauren Howe, Jon Jachimowicz, and Jochen Menges, "To Retain Employees, Support Their Passions Outside Work," *Harvard Business Review*, March 30, 2022, https://hbr.org/2022/03/to-retain-employees-support-their-passions-outside-work.

Chapter 24: Roll Forward or Roll Back

177 *an entrepreneur named Wayne Huizenga*: Gail DeGeorge, *The Making of a Blockbuster: How Wayne Huizenga Built a Sports and Entertainment Empire from Trash, Grit, and Videotape* (Wiley, 1996).

Chapter 25: Remember the Circle of Life

183 *the love of your own journey*: Ram Dass, "Death Is a Reminder to Live Fully," ramdass.org, May 6, 2014, https://www.ramdass.org/ram-dass-death-reminder-live-life-fully.

PHOTO: TESSA MOUL

About Chris Reynolds

CHRIS REYNOLDS started his career as a financial advisor because he loves working with people and helping them solve problems. This same passion motivated him to cofound Investment Planning Counsel as a firm built by advisors for advisors, with a client-first philosophy. More than thirty years later, his roles and responsibilities have evolved, but his fundamental interest in people and problem-solving remains as strong as ever. Chris focuses much of his energy on inspiring his team to create and embrace new opportunities in the wealth management industry, guided by evolving client needs. He also explores opportunities for advisors to build a better business through his *Turning the Page* podcast.

YOUR SIX CIRCLE JOURNEY STARTS HERE

My lifelong objective has been to help advisors build a better business through a remarkable client experience. I wrote *The Six Circle Strategy: The Entrepreneur's Journey to Wealth and Freedom* to help entrepreneurs learn from the mistakes and lessons I have learned over a thirty-year career in the wealth management industry, from starting a business from scratch to acquiring over twenty-six companies, then finally selling those businesses. If you are looking for a mentor in your entrepreneurial journey, I would be happy to help.

Listen to My Podcast

The *Turning the Page* podcast connects you with the leaders, the innovators, the people who are making it happen to inspire your personal and entrepreneurial growth. Join me to explore key insights from my experience as an entrepreneur, a buyer of businesses, an investor, and a mentor helping wealth entrepreneurs to succeed in every aspect of their business. *Turning the Page* is available on Spotify, Apple, and wherever you choose to listen to podcasts.

Build Your Career as an Advisor

As a company built by advisors for advisors, we are driven to support the growth of independent advisors across Canada. The Aspect, found at aspect.ipcc.ca, is where we share the knowledge we've gained and our thoughts about the future of the financial advice business. It's a space to share ideas and practical lessons from the field—and hopefully it becomes an aspect of your business and fuels new ideas and continued growth.

Invite Me to Speak

On stage, I speak from the perspective of my journey in hopes that it will inspire entrepreneurs to build better businesses by focusing on the most important thing: their client. Through my stories I bring audiences along on a journey to help them discover their own six circles and live their best lives every day. To book me for a speaking engagement, contact creynolds@ipcc.ca.

Tell Me What You Think

I'd love to hear what you've learned about your own entrepreneurial vision from reading *The Six Circle Strategy: The Entrepreneur's Journey to Wealth and Freedom*. And if you think the book might help others, drop me a positive review on Amazon, Google, or whichever retail site you like the most. It would really help get the word out.

Connect with Me Every Day

Don't stop asking questions. Give yourself permission to step right into a conversation with me. I'm online at www.linkedin.com/in/chrisreynoldsipc, and I'm open to hearing about your big idea.

Manufactured by Amazon.ca
Acheson, AB